Dear Zion

Dear Zion

Meditations for Zion Preachers & Other Preachers of the Gospel

Dr. Edward B. Saxon

WESTBOW
PRESS®
A DIVISION OF THOMAS NELSON
& ZONDERVAN

WestBow Press books may be ordered through booksellers or by contacting:

WestBow Press
A Division of Thomas Nelson & Zondervan
1663 Liberty Drive
Bloomington, IN 47403
www.westbowpress.com
1 (866) 928-1240

Scripture quotations from The Authorized (King James) Version. Rights in the Authorized Version in the United Kingdom are vested in the Crown. Reproduced by permission of the Crown's patentee, Cambridge University Press

ISBN: 978-1-9736-2196-6 (sc)
ISBN: 978-1-9736-2198-0 (hc)
ISBN: 978-1-9736-2197-3 (e)

Library of Congress Control Number: 2018902583

Print information available on the last page.

WestBow Press rev. date: 10/18/2018

CONTENTS

To my Sophia

FOREWORD

The circumstances of life have been navigated whereby I am part and parcel a product of the AME Zion ministry. My great Grand Father and Grand Mother were active members of the Small Memorial church in York, Pa. My paternal grandmother and her 7 children where active in the church as well. My Grandmother was the chief musician at Small Memorial. She started a touring singing group with her three sisters (also members of the church). When my father received his calling, he started his itinerate ministry at the John Wesley church in Harrisburg Pa. My dad also pastored the Wesley church in Chambersburg Pa. For close to thirty years he represented Zion as a Military chaplain in the armed forces recommended by Bishop Alfred Dunston. My maternal grandmother was a member of Big Wesley in Philadelphia Pa. She was an usher. The rest of her family lived in Salisbury NC. where they were all active members of the Soldiers Memorial AME Zion church. My uncle is a presiding elder in Mobile, and my other uncle who was Mayor of East Spencer NC was a Zion Preacher. My mother and father are graduates of Livingstone College. My wifes mother is a graduate of Livingstone College. My sister is a graduate of Livingstone College. My wife is a graduate of Livingstone College. I am a graduate of Livingstone College and my son is graduate of Livingstone College. When I received my calling, I started my ministry at the Pennsylvania Ave AME Zion church Baltimore MD. Dr. Marshall Strickland was both pastor and efficient mentor to me. I pastored 4 churches in Zion, two of which were very difficult churches. One Bishop referred to them as hornets nests. Yet I went because God called me and Bishop Strick Believed in me. I am very much aquatinted with the highs and lows of pastoring in Zion. At one appointment within one month we baptized 17 people. At another appointment, we brought in close to 70 in the first 6 months,(not bad for a midsized congregation). Our worship experiences have been ultra charismatic borrowing musicians from the apostolic church. Those are some of the highs. I have had members to hurt the church because they hated me. Me and my family have been literally thrown out on the street because of church politics. I have members refuse to pay me my salary because of power games. Those are the lows. At any rate, I have not come to weep and wail about how I have been treated good or bad. The ultimate purpose of tis document, is to emphatically tell pastors that its true…you can do all things through Christ that gives you strength! I have come to remind you dear local Pastor and Episcopal pastor that in the midst of whatever your going through, God is able. My prayer is that as you read this book that you are strengthened and empowered to be the best pastor and greatest preacher you can be. These are not the words of a novice or neophyte, these are the words from one who has lived the lyric. …

Stony the road we trod,
bitter the chastening rod,
felt in the day that hope unborn had died;
yet with a steady beat,
have not our weary feet,
come to the place on witch our fathers sighed?
we have come over a way that with tears has been watered,
we have come, treading our path through the blood of the slaughtered,
out from the gloomy past, till now we stand at last
where the white gleam of our bright star is cast.

With much much love,
Dr. Edward B. Saxon

CHAPTER 1

Getting It Back

*"Remember therefore from whence thou has fallen
and repent and do the first works" Revelations 2:5*

As I move towards maturity in my ecclesiology, I am consistently confronted with the prospect of an over-institutionalized church. The functionary machinations of the institution, the burdening bureaucracy of the organization, and the fervent maintenance of the corporation, transforms and transposes the Church from what it is meant to be, into something that is quite foreign. In such a church, policy and procedure outweigh power and proclamation, politics and personal favors are more important than mission and ministry, and getting to the top is more important than dealing with the least of these. In this scenario, setting and situation, the church begins to look like the institutionalized religion during the day of Jesus. Replete with 21st century scribes and Pharisees, the church begins to look like the institution, which gave Jesus the most trouble. In this chaotic and critical context it becomes difficult for a fresh anointing to fall. In this circumstance the movement of the Holy Ghost is aborted from the womb of human free will and authentic expression. In the end Jesus becomes locked out of the very church that he died to bring into existence. Our text is tailored to teach us that such was the case with Ephesus.

Ephesus certainly had a good start. In the text, the balanced perspective of the Prince of Peace begins by suggestively saying, *"I know your works"*. That alone ought be the crucial concern of every Pastor. *"I know your works"* That phrase alone speaks to motive, intent, and desire. The Ephesian church was austere and astute enough to try the preachers. They were destined, disciplined and determined enough to see who was flyin and who was lyin. At the bar of the altar the probing eye of the Episcopate would determine whether you were an Apostle or an apostate.

The Holy Orders committee had no friends when it came to determining who was real or who was fake. The candidate came **believing** that they were sent. The conference asked," *who sent you*"? Ephesus had a good start in the beginning because she tried the preachers. Ephesus had a good start because she endured hardship. Ephesus was not the easiest place to do ministry. She was a city of superstition. The city's patron god was Diana. Throughout the entire city there were trinkets made to honor Diana. When the Gospel began to spread, and people no longer desired Diana baubles and trinkets, the craftsmen got angry and stirred up a mob that threatened to kill the Apostle Paul. You could find a little bit of everything and anything in Ephesus.

Scholars sagaciously suggest that it was a morally depraved city. This was the environment that the church was placed in. One historian suggested that the inhabitants of the city were only worthy of drowning. The devotee of Diana obtained favor and oneness with the goddess by sleeping with her temple prostitutes. It was a morally depraved and despotic city. Yet in spite of its environment, the church is commended for labor that consisted of patience and perseverance. However something happened. As she labored fervently, her first love had waxed cold. The passionate blaze that had characterized her work and winsomeness had gone. She left her first love. At the outset of this passage it should be noted that the first love of any true Christian is not the institutional and mechanical ministry. It is possible to be deceived into believing that the faith relationship with God is exclusively about ministry.

To often we get hung up on ministries rather than the messiah of Christian ministry. The end result is that we overtly identify with religious institution as oppose to identifying with the person of Christ. At this point the faith community becomes the fan club of pulpit personalities, rather than bonified constituents of the kingdom. The first love is not the A.M.E., The A.M.E.Zion, the C.M.E, the COGIC, or the Baptist Church. Our public confession and lifestyle are bigger than the congregational assemblage, which takes place at 11: 00 on Sunday. The first love is bigger than a building program, more panoramic than a charismatic preacher and mightier than what is called a mega Church. Anyone who thinks that the faith is just about worship on Sunday morning is naïve. The first love of the Church triumphant and militant is none other than the dark child born in Bethlehem, Jesus Christ. The Ephesians willfully walked away from the sustaining principals of Jesus. The Ephesian church no longer received the teachings of Christ like she did before. She forgot that the church is a spiritual institution, not an institution of spirituality.

Like Gomer in the book of Hosea, her countenance changed as she left a loving husband for strange Johns in the red light district. She looked more like a corporation of men rather than the kingdom of God. She left her first love. She suffered spiritual A.D.D as her ultimate concern had to do with raising the general claim. Raising the budget became more important than winning souls. She left her first love. After all God did for her...delivering her from the task masters whip, saving her from the snarling and growling police dogs, getting her civil rights legislation, and allowing one of Africa's sons to become President of the United States, she never acknowledged her first love. Instead she made Gods of mere men, idols of entertainers, and worshiped reverently at the altar of a get rich at any cost capitalism. Alas, she left her first love.

Her spiritually amnesia caused her to forget the Lords words when he said, "*if you love me keep my commandments*". Her spiritual dementia caused her to forget the Lords words when he said, "*I am the vine and you are the branches*". Like the crowd in Mathew's Gospel who came to Jesus looking for a fish sandwich, or like the rich young ruler, that turned and walked away, she left her one true love. In the Greek, the word for *"left"* is a term that has to do with a wife leaving her good husband. One wonders what the repercussions are of a church that takes its Lord to divorce court. What is the repercussion of a church that tells the Lord *"I want nothing to do with you anymore"*? The answer is in the first part of the text. Jesus says in Essence, *" if you don't want me, I'll shut your church down. I will quickly come to you and remove the candlestick out of its place. **I will** stop people from joining your church and cause people to leave your church".* The risen Lord says, *" **I will** stop the giving and dry up the resources you have".* With authority in the tone and tenor of his voice he says, *"You will not act like a corporate CEO, you will not function like Fannie Mae or Freddie Mack. You will not hoodwink or bamboozle my people. My house shall be called a house of prayer. Anything short of this and you will be desolate".*

Well bro Saxon, what is the antidote? What steps do we need to take in order to regain and reclaim the favor and the fervor of the risen Lord? How can we get it back so hat our churches are growing again? How can we get it back so that we are financially strong again? What we gotta do? It's in the text. There is the possibility of progression based on the therapeutic advise of our Lord. He begins by suggesting that what really needs to happen is mental and intellectual transformation. The text says that the corporate mind of the church must change and they must **remembe**r where they came from. The term *"remember"* conveys the idea that a **re-membering**, or a re-connecting must take place. The idea is that they were once attached to something, they've become detached from something and now they must be reattached to what they became detached from. The risen Lord says, *"Remember where you came from"*.

He is calling them to remember that it was always more than the methodological approach of denominationalism. It was about loving God so much that one felt compelled to do Gods work. *"Remember from whence you have fallen"*. It use to be more than collecting the general claim. It use to be about making heavy investments in the stewards of the mysteries. *"Re-member from whence you have fallen"*. It use to be more than the black religious middle class process of church cloning and cookie cut worship experiences. It was about attracting the **whosoever will crowd**. *"Remember from whence you have fallen."* The church would sanctify time and space to talk to Her Lord. The origins of a theological heritage which embraced the totality of who we were as a people has been swapped for a Eurocentric theology handed to black people via a slave masters hand.

The clarion call is to remember from whence you have fallen. The sweet communion of community fellowship has been replaced by the rugged individualism of capitalism. *"Remember where you came from"*. It is from here that the risen Lord writes the second prescription. His diagnosis is such that Ephesus must not only re-member from whence they have fallen, but they must repent from what they are doing. In the native tongue of our Lord, the word repent would have connections with the historical straying of Israel from Yahweh. The idea behind the term is to feel sorrow for what one has done in the breeching and breaking of a covenant relationship. It is about making the journey back to God. Yet the Greek conveys the idea that even before the journey of returning to God takes place, one must *recognize* that they must "Get Back".

Hence the Greek word for repentance is interpreted as to *think anew*. The Apostle Paul would discuss matters of a renewed mind. Every church that struggles with institutional and organizational dysfunction must make the journey towards mind renewal. In the Latin, the intensified prefix is followed by a word, which means to punish. The self-inflicting punishment of non- productive thinking is freshly anointed thinking. Once again the etymological break down of the word suggest a spirit of grief over old thinking which has been futile. The risen Lord calls the church at Ephesus to repent. It is certainly ironic that when we hear this word repent we associate it with people that are outside the church. However repentance here is an in-house necessity. Sam Jeeva gives an appropriate illustration. It comes to us via the old Charlie Brown peanuts gang.

Several years ago, the peanuts comic strip had Lucy and Charlie Brown practicing football. Lucy was suppose to hold the ball for Charlie Brown, and Charlie Brown in turn was suppose to kick he ball. However every time Lucy would hold the ball for Charlie Brown, he would ferociously and fervently rush to kick the ball. At the point of no return Lucy would snatch the ball away from Charlie Brown, causing him to swoop up in the air and to fall flat on his back. On this occasion Lucy is holding the football for Charlie Brown to kick. Charlie Brown knows that if he makes the attempt to kick the ball, Lucy is just going to do what she always does. She is going to wait for Charlie Brown to run up and then she is going to remove the ball. Charlie Brown chooses not to kick the ball. Lucy begged him to kick the ball but Charlie brown refuses to kick the ball. Charlie Brown said *"Every time I try to kick the ball you move it and I fall flat on my back'*.

They went back and forth over this until Lucy broke down in tears. She said, *" Charlie Brown, I have been so terrible to you over the years picking up the football when you get ready to kick it. I have played so many tricks on you. However, I have seen the error of my ways. I could see the hurt look in your eyes when I have deceived you. I have been wrong.... so wrong. Won't you give a poor penitent girl another chance"*? Charlie Brown was so moved with compassion that he said, *"Of course I'll give you another chance."* He stepped back as she held the ball. With all his might he ran to kick the ball and.... Lucy removed the ball again! Listen to Lucy's theology. *"Recognizing your faults and changing your ways are two different things"!* Every time we think that the sermon is more about us than saving souls, we snatch the ball away!

Every time we want to be recognized for the beautiful solo we sung, instead of giving God the glory, we snatch the ball away. Every time we spend more time fighting leadership as oppose to supporting good leadership, we snatch the ball away. Unfortunately, many churches are left lying on their back because there are two many negativities that love snatching the ball away. However Lucy has good theology, *recognizing your faults and changing your behavior are two different things.* The risen Lords calls Ephesus A.M.E.Zion Church To remember whence they have fallen. The risen Lord calls Ephesus to repent from what they are doing, and finally the Risen Lord calls them to repeat what they use to do. He says do the first works. Getting it back would be no introspective theological journey. Theology would develop into praxis as they are called to remember, repent, and re-do. The call to remember coupled with the act of repentance would cause the church to be a *doing* church. The formula of remembering, repenting, and redoing would stop the church from re-crucifying Christ through their blatant disrespect and dislike of the man or woman of God. They would move from being a dead church to a doing Church. The formula would stop them from singing songs in such a depressing way that the sweet melody of salvific themes is so oft drowned in an ocean of apathy. The self-gratifying practice of massaging the ego of the status quo would turn to the extended hand reaching out to the least of these. They would become a doing church rather than a dead church. They would be a living church, and living churches are what we need the most. Remember!! Repent!! Re-do!!!

CHAPTER 2

Fearless and Faithful

"Fear none of those things which thou shall suffer. Behold the devil shall cast some of you in prison that you may be tried, and you shall have tribulation for ten days. Be thou faithful unto death and I will give you the crown of life". Revelations 2:10"

It was a cool evening in Glen Burnie Maryland when I received a phone call. The voice on the other end was authoritative yet gentle. The voice was strange but familiar. It was the voice of one of Zion's great Bishops. I will never forget the content of that conversation. *"Saxon, there is a church that is in need of good strong Pastoral leadership in Tuscaloosa Alabama. The church has a membership of about 125 and I need somebody in there to bless the work"*. After I prayed about it, I made my way to Tuscaloosa. I stayed at the Masters inn hotel. The next day the Presiding Elder made his way to the hotel and introduced himself to me. He took me out to lunch. Reflecting on this time makes me laugh to myself as I am convinced that the veteran Elder silently said, "*This guy is so green* ". At any rate we finished up the last bit of our lunch, wiped our mouths, paid the check, and headed to my new appointment.

I was so excited about pastoring a great church in a historical city. As we made the sojourn to the great Zion church we passed many churches. Each church created a rise of excitement in my spirit. We passed a large Methodist church with a commanding structure. In my spirit I said. "*This is the one.... Yes*"! However the fire of my excitement was dowsed as we continued driving pass the church. We drove to another church on the campus of Stillman College. I got excited again. I said, "Yeah.... *I'm going to be a campus Pastor*"! Fantasies developed in my mind about how I was going to minister to students at an HBCU. However the fire of my passion was assuaged as we drove pass this church as well. As I looked out the window of the long drive, I noticed that the cosmopolitan metropolis began to change. Big buildings turned into trees.... so many trees.

Downtown colleges and campuses turned into farms. Suddenly my "*Yes*" turned into " **oh -no**". As the drive took a little longer than expected, I asked myself, "*Where in Gods name is this man taking me*"? As we finally pulled up to the church, we were both greeted by the odoriferous scent of cow manure. The melodious musical mooing of the cows were heard around the place of spiritual domicile, as with shirt and tie I watched little piglets run across the property. When I finally met with the officers of the church, I discovered that they didn't have an astronomical budget. In fact the amount they payed the Pastor was ten times less than what I was making before I arrived. It was really at this point that I was ready to decline the appointment, and rescind my resignation. At any rate I discovered that much good would come from my so-called shattered expectation. The Episcopate was very pastoral. The Presiding Elder was the best Presiding Elder I ever had. The brothers and sisters on the district were some of the finest people I had ever known. The church proved to be the most peaceful and serene appointment that I ever pastored. It was a good appointment. It didn't have all of the trappings of what is referred to as a silk stocking appointment. It didn't really have a lot of financial resources, but it was a good church. I guess I mention this because every time I read this passage in the apocalypse, The Beautiful Zion A.M.E. Zion Church experience comes to mind. Whenever I read this passage the midsized congregation that struggles to do meaningful ministry with meager resources comes to mind.

I think about the pastor who desires to do great things for God at the local level, and who facing all kinds of obstacles forges his or her way through to do the will of God. When I think of this passage I think of the trustee who strives to demonstrate love for God and love for the pastor. I think of the steward who out of a desire to see the church flourish is creative in finding resources so that the ministry will not only only strive but will thrive. I reflect upon the quiet demeanor of a member who just wants to hear a word from the Lord. This is precisely what the church at Smyrna looked like. Smyrna was a bustling city, which boasted of being one of the greatest cities in the empire. It was the one city, which was destroyed, but who came back to life under the leadership of Alexander the great. As it was notorious for its fine wines, it was a city of culture.

It possessed the finest libraries and theaters. Yet while it was a city nestled in a strategic position militaristically, while it was a paradise for the lovers of municipal organization and involvement, it was a hot bed for what was referred to then as Ceaser worship. The empire had been good to its inhabitants. The city that had been leveled by military conquest, rose from the smoldering ash heaps of war. The sea had been safe from pirates, the Pax Romano was in effect, and the economy was thriving. However in an attempt to solidify the loyalty of the people along with the unity of the city-states the idea was lifted up that the greatness of Rome was personified and deified in the Roman emperor. In other words, the greatness of Rome was personified in a person who they thought was worthy of worship. The greatest mistake a preacher can make is to subtly believe he/she has the right to be worshiped.

When a preacher is consistently called to run revival, when he/she is called to be the conference preacher, when he or she is on the lecture circuit, the enemy easily manipulates the mind into thinking its all about him/her. I believe it was Bishop John R. Bryant who gleefully went to his father Bishop Bryant senior and told him how great of a church experience he had. He said he told his father how well everything went. People were joining, there were no major issues, and the people loved him.

His father responded, *"You've built a good fan club, now go back and build a church"*. What a word of wisdom! Today we have more fan clubs than churches. The Roman emperor was deified. He was seen as one who must be worshiped. They were to burn incense and say, *"Caesar is lord"*. The church at Smyrna had a problem with that because there was one Lord and his name was Jesus. Hence they were perceived as being revolutionaries. Homes were broken into, family members were hunted down like dogs, and many men and women were killed. That was the threat from the outside. The threat from the inside came from what the risen Lord refers to as the Synagogue of Satan. There was a church subculture amidst the church culture. The only distinguishable difference was that the subculture church was not a church at all. It was a devil church.

At the most basic and elementary understanding, this church desired to turn the church into something that it was not designed to be. Foreign beliefs were introduced to the infant church, which threatened the doctrinal integrity of the community of believers. At any rate the risen Lord commends Smyrna efforts for not cowering and assimilating to the surrounding culture. He further gives the prescription for her survival. On the one hand he commands her to be fearless. He encourages them to not be afraid. It is certainly ironic that the phrase *be not afraid* shows up 365 times in the bible. There is a *be not afraid* for every day out of the year including leap year. What is of most importance is the level of authority the one who is saying it has, and further- more what the connection is between what is spoken and the experiences that we go through on a personal level.

A shaking man cannot tell other men not to be afraid. Recognizing that an individual is in control over what fear does to him or her, the risen Lord reminds us that God has no formidable foe, and because God has no formidable foe, there is no reason to be afraid. Stress which comes from the uncertainty of knowing whether or not you will be returning to the Pastorate for another year, the depression which springs upon you over not having enough salary to take care of your family, wondering whether you have what it takes to be a good pastor represents the darkness in which the bright words illuminate the most abysmal circumstances and situations.

The risen Lord says, "*don't be afraid*". The risen lord is not delusional to the angel of the church at Smyrna. Jesus was very open about what they would go through. He said, "*They will through some of you in prison. They will take some of you to court. You will suffer miserably for ten days straight*". Jesus was crystal clear about what they would be up against. Before appointing me to a particular station, I had a Bishop who was very upfront with me regarding the character of the church. He said, "*Edward, this church hates preachers. They love to make fools out of preachers. It's a hornets nest*". His words to me were, "*I'm putting you there because I know you're not afraid of nothing*". In a sense the Lord was telling the angel and the church this would not be a plush congregation. This will not be an experience where all is sweet and serene. Every Pastor ought to know that not all pastorates will be flagship appointments.

You will not always pastor the great church on the urban boulevard. The Lord is upfront with the angel of the church. What is most significant is this is not a freshly planted church.

This is an already established church. The forecast isn't promising. The prophetic word is not one of prosperity, and the promise isn't positive. One is forced to evaluate ones character by asking the reflective question, " *would I go to that church if the Bishop told me the same thing*"? What if the Bishop came to me saying, "*I'm going to send you to a church where they will do everything in their power to throw you in prison, You will always be in and out of court, And then you will have a season of miserable suffering*". I am quite sure in our generation; many of us would run in the opposite direction. Yet within the context of this correspondence the Lord doesn't say, "*I'll fight your battle*". He doesn't promise to destroy the enemy. He says, " *don't be afraid*". When the pastorate becomes a furnace that has been turned up to the seventh degree, to the pastor in the midst of his or her private pain, comes a whisper in the darkest of midnights, which prays the Gethsemane prayer. (If it is possible, let this cup pass from me) It is at this point that the Lord says, " *Don't be afraid*".

My mother use to tell me about one night when it was time for me to go to bed. When she turned the lights out and shut the door, I became terrified. The whimpering sounds of a scared child could be heard down the hall. When my Dad came into the room, he sat by my bed and said, "*Don't be afraid because there is nothing to be afraid of*". It was not just the voice that spoke, it was the presence coupled with the voice.

My father didn't shout it from another room. He didn't say it from downstairs, he didn't face book it, he didn't text it, and he didn't tweet it. However the presence behind the voice was right in the darkness with me. Every Pastor ought to know, trust and believe, that there is presence behind the voice. To the Pastor who struggles year after year to keep the mission moving and consistently gets shot down by vision impaired members, the voice of his presence says, "*Don't be afraid*". To the Bishop who is Holy Ghost passionate about taking the conference to the next Level, but struggles with know it all preachers, the risen Lord says, "*Don't be afraid*".

To the pastor who has lost the church and feels like the canary in the canyon the risen Lord says, " *Don't be afraid*". We discover in this text that we are not only called to be fearless, but we are called to be faithful. Imagine that! Amidst a church that is going through traumatic and dramatic dysfunction, Jesus simply encourages us to be fearless and faithful. The word here for faithful is translated better "*reliable*". How interesting it is that the God, which we so heavily rely upon, is relying on us. I am convinced that the whole God - church relationship is permeated through the act of reciprocity. We depend on God and God depends on us. The introspective question that ought to reside in our heart is, *how dependable am I*? Can God depend on me to show up at our morning and evening appointment so that God can tell me what to preach? Can God depend on me to be fearless and faithful in my preaching no matter what the cost is? Can God depend on me to be committed to the faith and teachings of the Gospel when I am in church and when I am away? Can God depend on me not to prey on the women or not to fool with the men in the church? How dependable am I? Can God depend on me to be committed to the word in my leadership? How reliable am I? When an ornery member storms into the office to cuss you out and tell you off, can God depend on you to be an example of patience and self-control? When the Pastor is without a pulpit, can God depend on you to trust that in the end a Bishop gives a piece of paper but the Lord gives the assignment?

Can the Lord depend on you? When the good pastor walks away from congregational wars at members meeting only to walk into rejection at home, can the Lord trust the good pastor to maintain his/her integrity and dignity as a pastor? Con sider the following illustration. An eagle can reach superior heights and then nose dive of up to 150 miles per hour. As she stretches her wide and majestic wings this mighty monarch of the stars soars upward, and then with pierced eyes and the wind pushing back her feathers, she dives. As she is in the heart of her dive, she snatches a branch, holds it in her mouth and then spits it out. Why does she do this? When she is courting the male eagle, she wants to make sure that he is quick enough to catch the branch in mid air. If he is going to be a daddy eagle, when the mommy eagle kicks the baby eagle out of the nest to teach him how to fly, she has to depend on daddy eagle to catch the baby eagle before it hits the ground. The Lord our God soars high and in his ascent he snatches of areas of responsibility. He looks to see who is diligent enough, who is spiritual enough, who is committed enough to catch the church from his mouth.

Yes, the song rings true! The road gets rough, the going gets tough, and the hills are hard to climb. I started out a long time ago and there is no doubt in my mind. The poison of skepticism has not intellectually destabilized me in the matters of faith. The prognosis of the problem is perplexing. The analytical assessment of the adversity is antagonizing, yet I've decided to make Jesus my choice. My intellectual conviction mingled with my emotional passion has shaped and formed my will, I have decided to make Jesus my choice!

"Amidst the turbulent and buoyant moments of life, I Know I can depend on God. Whether in the valley or on the violent sea, he watches over me. Amidst the desolate desert of joyless moments, never refreshed by the sun rain of laughter blossoming the beauty of a radiant smile, I can depend on God. Amidst ripped up relationships, finished finances, and a feeble frame, I can depend on God. . Can God depend on me, to open my mouth and speak of eternity? Can God depend on me to share and tell that the gift of God is free? Can God depend on you, to share that his word is true"?

O for a commitment that says:

My faith looks up to thee.. thou Lamb of Calvary, Savior divine! Now hear me while I pray, take all my guilt away, O let me from this day be wholly thine! .

May thy rich grace impart strength to my fainting heart, my zeal inspire!

As thou hast died for me, O may my love to thee pure, warm, and changeless be, a living fire!

While life's dark maze I tread, and griefs around me spread be thou my guide; bid darkness turn to day, wipe sorrows's tears away,nor let me ever stray from thee aside

When ends life's transient dream, when death's cold, sullen stream shall o'er me roll blest Savior, then in love, fear and distrust remove; O bear me safe above a ransom soul

CHAPTER 3

The Sword of His Mouth

*"Repent.. or I will come unto thee quickly,
and will fight against them with the sword
of my mouth"* **Revelations 2:16**

*I*t is easily assumed that the church is supposed to be the place of ethereal peace, blessed tranquility, and unbroken unity. There are many who come to church believing that this is the way church is, and this is the way church ought to be. There are many who have been in the church for a long time, yet whom the least bit of church conflict shakes. At any rate I believe I am on solid ground when I note that the perfect church does not exist on this side of glory. In fact I have discovered that the church is the place where spiritual warfare is most fierce. The gates of hell may not prevail, but that does not mean that they will not try. I have learned that the church, which doesn't experience some level of conflict and contention, may need to look at the level of ministry that they are at. Organizational dynamics teach us that conflict will occur. As a footnote to this let me suggest that church conflict is not just cultural.

Both black and white churches experience conflict. Conflict is not just logistical.. Big churches and little churches experience church conflict. Conflict is not just organizational. Denominational and non- denominational churches experience conflict. What is most significant is the nature of the conflict. The faith community at Pergamum represents the nature of the conflict that most churches experience. In the text we discover that there are two warring factions. On the one hand there are those that are faithful. In spite of the negative environment that the Christians of Pergamum find themselves in, they remain faithful. My how times have changed! In this generation members are often enticed and encouraged to leave their church at the least bit of trouble.

The fact is that during this time the church was more than a place of worship. The church at this time was a community in every sense of the word. One could no more leave their community of faith than they would just walk away from their family. Problem filled or problem free, the church was their family. They were faithful. There was no power tripping, there was no pastor bashing, and there was no political jockeying among this crowd because they were faithful. In spite of external pressure to identify with the world, in spite of the death of loved ones, in spite of a bleak outlook regarding relief from a bad situation, they remained faithful. That was one part of the membership. They paid their tithe, they attended bible study, they supported the vision, and they went the extra mile. They were faithful. On the other hand there were some other folk in Pergamum A.M.E.Zion Church.

They are characterized in two ways. On the one hand the Risen Lord says there are those who hold the teaching of Balaam in the Old Testament. (Numbers 22-24, Numbers 31:8, 16)

King Balak of Moab wanted to do the children of Israel harm. He didn't want to use regular weapons, he wanted to use psychological warfare. As the narrative goes, he called on Balaam, (a diviner) to curse the children of Israel. Balak sent dignitaries and great wealth in order to convince Balaam. As Balaam was about to go, the angel of the Lord stopped him. His heart wasn't right and the angel prevented him from going forth. However God changed his mind and told Balaam that he could go but he could only speak what God told him to speak. While Balaam's purpose was to curse the people of God, God made it so that only blessings flowed from his mouth.

At any rate, when Balaam realized there was no pay in speaking blessings, he devised another plan. Balaam encouraged the king to allow the people of God to assimilate into Midian and Moabite culture, which would cause a self inflicted curse upon them. The children of Israel married into the culture, committed fornication, and began serving idol Gods. It cost the people of God 24,000 lives. The secret counsels that Balaam gave to Balak caused lives to be lost. Balaam got broke off, but Gods people got broke down. Balaam got paid but Gods people got slayed. There are people that are in the church only for what they can get out of it. They don't care about the identity of the church, the mission of the church, the integrity of the church, or about the development and growth of the church. In many connectional situations and scenarios, the modus operand for this group boils down to power and money.

One works fervently in a given position to get power, or one works fervently in a position to get paid. The casualties of this ethic are church carcasses wounded on a dying district. Balaam forgot that the decisions that one makes have long term affects on the people one serves. Well Pergamum not only had Balaamites, the risen Lord said they had Nicolations. At the outset it must be suggested that the primary problem with this group was that they were involved in doctrinal belief that the Lord literally hated. It is significantly important for all church members to evaluate the nature of their doctrine against the standard set by Jesus himself. Our doctrinal belief is more than the passing fad and fashion of a consistently changing culture. Our doctrinal belief is a matter of life and death. Far be it that we should live a lifetime possessing a doctrine that Jesus hates. At any rate, to better understand the doctrine of this crowd one must look at the commentary of the early church fathers.

Historically, biblical scholarship divides along two lines of thought. On the one hand, there are those who believe that Nicolas started the sect. (Nicolas was one of the seven deacons selected by the apostles).

The idea is that Nicolas strayed from the faith and there were many who followed him. The group is notorious for showing up in other churches. The second line of thought is that Nicolas did not start this movement but the wicked members of the movement adopted his name to gain acceptance among the true believers. While there is much debate about the origins of the movement, there is apostolic and historical consensus regarding the character and doctrine of the Nicolatians. The Constitutions of the Holy Apostles states that "*those who are falsely called Nicolaitians are impudent in uncleanness.*" Tertullian says, "*The Nicolaitians, in their maintenance of lust and luxury, destroy the happiness of sanctity.*" Irenaeus writes, "They *lead lives of unrestrained indulgence, and teach it is a matter of indifference to practice adultery, and to eat things sacrificed to idols.*" Ignatius brands them as "*lovers of pleasure, and given to slanderous speeches. They affirm that unlawful unions are a good thing, and place the highest happiness in pleasure.*"

It is clear that the Nicolatiaons were an internal threat to the Pergamum Church. Pergamum possessed a sub Church culture in the midst of the Church. The faithful had to deal with the Balaamite and Nicolatian crowd. During the worship experience, one side of the church would be shouting to the glory of God, while the other side just sat with their arms folded. The faithful would grace the church for bible study, but this other crowd would always make illegitimate excuses. The faithful would spread the Gospel; this other crowd would spread the gossip. The faithful believed in having productive church meetings. This other crowd hosted secret meetings. The faithful would lift up their pastor. This other crowd would consistently tear pastor down. This is what the angel of Pergamum had to deal with. At this point it must be noted that the expectation of the risen Lord was not to cajole the Balaamites or the Nicolations. The risen Lord did not expect the angel of the church to pander to the Balaamites and Nicolations because they were big tithers. There was no expectation of trying to butter them up for fear that they could cause the angel to lose his or her appointment. The risen Lord does not call us to hug a rattlesnake, or to pet a scorpion. This needs to be mention because in many connectional churches the idea is pushed to get the budget at any cost. Don't argue with them or destroy the church, just get the assessment. Revelation 2:16 does not agree with that leadership model.. The risen Lord is angry because the angel keeps the church in an unproductive unchanged state. In the text, the risen Lord says, *"Either you have the courage to deal with them, or I'm going to deal with them"*. The word of the Lord is that if Pergamum church doesn't repent, he will come quickly and fight them with the sword of his mouth.

To come quickly with the sword is reflective of Roman Jurisprudence. The Roman Governor (and sometimes the Roman soldier) had the authority to execute someone on the spot. The ius gladi was the right to exact the death penalty in a moment's notice. One of the reasons why Simon of Cyrene helped Jesus carry the cross was because he knew that if he refused, the Roman praetorian had the right to kill him on the spot. Justice was exacted with a quick fierceness. This is a message of Judgment from the risen Christ. It is a message not just to the holders of the false doctrine, but it is a message to those who hold the holders of false doctrine. In this sense, the word of God (which is a sword), merely becomes a proclamation which sentences a church to death.

Every angel of the church ought to take a close look at the congregation and ask themselves, *"Are there members in the church that are putting the church on death row"*? At the final hour will she be denied a reprieve because her tolerance for sin is lackadaisical and accommodating? I have found that there are two ways to deal with the Balaamites and Nicolatians On the one hand the angel must gracefully convince them. Balaamites andNicolatians at least needed to be afforded the opportunity to see the error of their ways. A level of sympathy ought to be felt towards those who have received bad teaching and those who have been misled. Amidst a congregation that was dysfunctional and in disarray, Bishop Daryl Starnes stood before a motley crew and apologized for all of the bad teaching they received throughout the years. One of the reasons why an angel of the church must be an able teacher is because he or she must often take members through the process of intellectual and spiritual re-tooling.

For many members Balaam and Nicolatian theology is all they know. They have not been afforded the rich experience of engaging the stretching horizons of theological development. They are comfortable with milk, and afraid of meat. In this situation, teaching is the preferred prescription. On the other hand one must remember that all Balaamites and Nicolations will not receive gracious convincing. It is at this point that the angel must aggressively combat the spirit of rebellion that is within them. They must fight them with the sword of the word.

Hebrews notes that the word of God is a double edge sword piercing and boring its way through to the secret intents of the heart. They must fight because the church is at stake. They must fight because the angel is held accountable. They must fight because the risen Lord is depending on them.

CHAPTER 4

Ministering to Jezebel

*Behold, I will cast her into a bed, and them that
commit adultery with her into great tribulation,
except they repent of their deeds. And I will kill
her children with death; and all the churches
shall know that I am he which searcheth the reins
and hearts: and I will give unto every one of you
according to your works".. Revelation 2:22-23*

The correspondence to each church in Revelation has
a pattern of theological nomenclature as it relates to
the ministers of each church. The minister is not referred to
as *pastor*. The ministers are referred to as *angels*. The better
translation is messenger. The ecclesiological understanding is
that the minister of the Gospel is always more of a *messenger*
than a *pastor*. The pastorate is established through the ministry
of the word. The angelion is at the root of the ecclesia. If there

is no messenger there is no ministry. The messenger at Thyatira had a unique context. One could sufficiently say that the context was a good context. The risen Lord accentuates the nature of this contextual arrangement. On the one hand the church had hard workers. This was not a lazy church. The ministry was not conclusive of Sunday morning worship at 11:00. This was not the scope of their entire ministry.

They were a working church. The church had an active mission and was led by an active visionary. It was a working church. Thyatira was not a dead church. It was active in the worship, active in the membership, and active in the community. This was a working church. Thyatira was not only a working church but it was a loving church. The risen Lord commends their charity. This was not a church that sat on top of its economic resources and bid everyone who passed by the great cathedral to look at them. This was a loving church. The economic resources were poured into community programs.

The homeless feeding program took place just before the worship experience on Sunday. The *Maat* mentoring program happened each weeknight for young black men. The sisters in the spirit group met each Tuesday and Thursday night. The seniors club received new computers for seniors in cyberspace. The angel food ministry was off the chain. Many members who had been burned out, or who could not afford to keep their lights on were helped. Thyatira was a loving church. Thyatira was a church of faith.

Many times they did not know how they were going to make it. The tithes and offerings were low and the bills kept coming in. However Thyatira church knew how to trust in the Lord. There were no whining stewards, or negative trustees. They knew how to trust the Lord. Thyatira was a patient church. They didn't interrogate and judge non-church members when they came in. They didn't complain that her dress was to short or that he walks like a girl. They didn't pounce on him because his pants were sagging, or look down on her because she had tattoos. They were patient enough to work with them in the process of total transformation. The messenger at Thyatira was privileged to serve in a great context. However in Thyatira, the messenger of God had to deal with another messenger. It is textually obvious that this other messenger put the mess in messenger. The other messenger is referred to as Jezebel. She is seen as the spiritual re-incarnation of the Jezebel in the Old Testament. Transference occurs as Manipulation, influence and vindictiveness characterize this New Testament Jezebel. Her aforementioned character traits put her at odds with the risen Lord. These would be the traits, which would affect the overall ministry of Thyatira. It is essential for every messenger of the risen Lord to understand that Jezebel has not gone anywhere. Jezebel in reality has nothing to do with gender, but has everything to do with character or the lack thereof. Jezebel underhandedly undermines the work of Gods visionary. Jezebel is the one who secretly whispers and gossips about other members in the church. Jezebel is the one who holds un- official secret meetings in her house. Jezebel is the one who refuses to pay the assessment even when she has the money to do so. Jezebel makes fools out of preachers. She is manipulative vindictive, influential, and dictatorial. Jezebel is a control freak. Jezebel doesn't care about leading people; she is just interested in people following her. Jezebel is a conformist, and teaches others to be conformist. The ironic thing here is that the angel of Thyatira put this person in a position to teach. Perhaps, at an earlier time they were in good fellowship. Perhaps earlier she demonstrated traits and skill, which would be beneficial to the church. Perhaps earlier she was an ally. She was appointed in good faith by the angel of the church, however in time the angel would notice a shift in her attitude.

As the pastor preached and proclaimed with the power of the paraclete, her posture in the pew was both cynical and sinister. The familiar doctrines that the angel of Thyatira taught her began vanishing as her teachings were becoming strange. She taught untouched by the chief teacher or messenger of the Lord. In the text the risen Lord points out the root of the problem. As the church is becoming impacted by her false teaching, the messenger of the risen Lord at Thyatira is afraid to confront Jezebel. The risen Lord says, *"You have a relationship of tolerance with her"*. The real question becomes, "why is the messenger of the risen Lord afraid to confront Jezebel? Is it an avoidance -approach scenario? Is he or she afraid of the dualistic negative goal out come? (If I let her go, she'll take the money…if I don't let her go she'll break up the church). Why is the angel afraid to confront Jezebel?

Does the fear of confrontation stem from an upbringing of always wanting to be accepted? Does it come from the good Rev's innate desire to go along to get along? Is he afraid to upset the applecart? Why is the angel of Thyatira afraid to confront Jezebel? Is he or she an imposing Buxton intimidating figure? The risen Lords' overall analysis of the matter, the consistent question to the messenger of the Lord is *"Reverend...what will you do with Jezebel? Will you continue to let her disrupt the church with her false teaching? What will you do with Jezebel"*? The question is asked to every pastor in the year 2017. Notice the nature of the problem. Because there is no confrontation there is assimilation. Jezebels ministry contributed to the church losing its identity. She taught them to be sexually immoral and to eat food offered to idols. The greatest challenge to pastoral ministry is to keep the church from losing its identity.

The criticism of black church scholars is that too much western influence has come upon the black church. The institution, which was known for speaking truth to power, has dwindled down to the flighty proclamations of motivational speakers. Jezebel was a threat to the churches identity. Jezebel was placed into a position where she had the qualifications of the world but she didn't live according to the word. Jezebel may have an accounting degree but that didn't qualify her as a steward. Jezebel may have been a relator but that didn't qualify her to be a trustee. Jezebel may have been a gifted musician, but that didn't qualify her to be a church musician. Jezebel may be a seminary graduate but that doesn't qualify her to be a preacher of the gospel. The desecration of the sacred office occurs when one selfishly leads followers towards the loss of identity and down the primrose path of destruction... and this is where the heart of the problem was.

Somehow Jezebel got the confidence of the pastor and was able to get into a position, which was harmful to the congregation. At this point it should be noted that a congregation that has too many Jezebels will not grow in ministry.

The enemy puts Jezebel in productive churches to stunt the mission of the fellowship. God help the pastor who is sent to pastor a congregation of Jezebels. . Again, this has nothing to do with gender. This has everything to do with those acomadationalist who are demonically possessed to redefine the church and bring about its destruction. The Thyratirian messenger of the risen Lord does not confront Jezebel. The Thyratirian messenger of the risen Lord tolerates Jezebel. In other words, Jezebel does what she wants to do, and the messenger of the risen Lord suffers. Much in the area of contemporary pastoral theology suggests that the pastor ought to let Jezebel do what she wants to do. Our churches are literally turned upside down and inside out because too many pastors let Jezebel do what she wants to do.

As long as the pastor's salary is paid, as long as they raise the claim, as long as they give me a slammin appreciation, Jezebel can do whatever she wants to do. What's the good Rev. to do? A close look at the text will reveal an interruption by the risen Lord. It is not so much what he wants his messenger to do. In the text the Lord deals directly with the problem crowd. He begins by suggesting that he gave Jezebel a chance. The grace and the mercy of the risen Lord is extended even to Jezebel. The love of the Lord for Jezebel suggests that he even wants Jezebel to change so that Jezebel can be used in the kingdom. The text does not suggest that the risen Lord wants Jezebel fired from her position. The risen Lord gives her a chance to change. Grace and mercy are ways of ministering to Jezebel.

Perhaps Jezebel does not understand the magnitude of her behavior. Maybe Jezebel is the product of bad teaching. Maybe she needs to be taught. The risen Lord extends grace and mercy to her. Perhaps Jezebel has zeal but no knowledge. Maybe she's just excited to be teaching. Pastor have you talked to Jezebel? Do you have a relationship with Jezebel? Does Jezebel respect you enough to listen to you and not just hear you? To what extent have you trained Jezebel? Have you showed her how to teach and what to teach in a loving way? Or maybe you have had a consistent combative relationship with her. Maybe it's always been about you and not about the ministry. Maybe you distance yourself away from her because she refuses to be your little flunky.

Have you talked to Jezebel? Have you reached out to Jezebel? What has been the model of your ministerial approach to the challenge of Jezebel? Have you talked to Jezebel? In the text the risen Lord says, *"I have given her a chance. However, although I have given her a chance, she did not act upon that chance. She continued in the bad behavior"*. The risen Lord warns Jezebel. She is out of compliance with the word of God. She is working outside of his will, and except she repents she will experience the fullness of his wrath. After you have loved on Jezebel, and after you have tried to teach Jezebel, the time comes when you must warn Jezebel. Jezebel must be warned about the consequences of her behavior.

Now understand the consequences go far beyond taking an appointment from Jezebel Taking an appointment won't change the behavior. In fact, Jezebel may go to the Zion church down the street. Taking her appointment is lite work. Taking an interest to the point of warning of disastrous peril is another matter. This is not a warning about what the messenger will do; it is a warning about what God will do. Just because Jezebel looses her teaching post does not mean that Jezebel will become inactive in the church. Lifting the appointment is lite work. The real work comes when as the leader; you love the assailant enough to remind them in love, "*if you don't stop, then God will stop you*". As the leader, the messenger has the ability to take the appointment.

God has the authority to take the life. The risen Lord threatens to exact the pain on Jezebel and her followers in order to make an example of them. In a sense the risen Lord says, "*I have to make an example of you so that the churches on the district will know that there are some things I won't tolerate*". Finally I am convinced that Jezebel has been planted inside Of many small churches The church at Thyatira is the smallest church on the Asian district, and Jezebels desire to dismantle the church is to get them to become a part of immoral and idolatrous trade union guilds that were operative in Thyatira. In other words her values do not evolve from the context of the church. Her values are informed by false religion masquerading as business unions. The point is that Jezebels tend to show up in smaller weaker congregations. In some cases the membership is not astute or resourceful enough to ward off the bogus teachings of Jezebel. This is why messengers who pastor smaller churches must be vigilant. Jezebel will not only cause the preacher to have a nervous breakdown, Jezebel will not only cause the congregation to be grief stricken, but Jezebel will cause he congregation to split with more than half the members walking away from the church. The interesting thing about this text is that although Jezebel is seducing the congregation in a negative way, the risen Lord sees a remnant. Often the boisterous Jezebel crew does not intimidate the remnant. They are not intimidated by Jezebel's seemingly exhaustive knowledge of church things. She knows the law of the church, she knows the tradition of the church, and sometimes she is aware of the theology of the church. All of this becomes a manipulative tool in her box of wickedness. Yet the text suggests that there is a remnant. One of the mistakes I made at one pastoral appointment was I concentrated on the wickedness of Jezebel instead of focusing on the remnant of the Lord. I was in a workshop with Bishop Walter Scott Thomas. In the workshop he noted that if a sermon is 45 minuets long, why give Jezebel and her crew 30 minuets of sermon time? God condemns the wicked, but works through the remnant. Whatever happened to Jezebel in the Old Testament? The book says that she was destroyed by Gods remnant who where in her own house. The clarion call of the leader is to mobilized forces that Jezebel doesn't even know about. When all is said and done, the words of Jesus ring true. Upon this rock will I build my church, and the gates of hell shall not prevail.

CHAPTER 5

The Church That
Was Frontin

*"Be watchful, and strengthen the things which
remain, that are ready to die"…..Revelations 3; 2*

 I sit in my favorite chair in the living room. I flip through
the stations engaging in the familiar yet colloquial
terminology called channel surfing. My thumb stops moving
at a particular channel. On the T.V., I see a worship service. The
preacher is fervently preaching, and as sweat drips down his
facial expression of excitement and energy, the crowd of 7000 is
in an uproar. Some of the members are so excited that they leap
up out of their seat with dollars in hand and literally through
them at the preachers' feet. I watch the membership run around
the church, and some are even dancing in the isle. To the young
preacher who is starting out in his/her ministerial stride, this

formation becomes the inner context that shapes his or her objectives and goals. This becomes their ultimate concern. This becomes their aspiration. What the neophyte preacher doesn't understand is that everything is not always as it seems.

The church in this generation seems to be ideologically locked into a mental construct, which says that the successful church is the church that has the largest membership, the best choir, and the most charismatic preacher. In this generation the T.V. church becomes the standard for what successful ministry is. The real question becomes, "Are we genuinely able to suggest what church is or is not successful"? There is always a difference between seeing and knowing. We see what is in the front of us, but we don't always know what is going on in the life of that church. Our assumptions are based on what we see, not always on what we know. Often our narrow understanding of church is based on our selfish experience in church. (if it does nothing for me, then its no good)

The extent of the faith walk for many is just to show up at the Sunday morning worship. Experiencing a dynamic worship service doesn't mean that all is well. With our finite, limited, blurry view, are we really able to say what church is or is not successful? In the end we discover that it is not so much about how people see our church, it is about what God says about our church. The word of the risen Lord literally snatches the covers off of what is happening at Sardis. You have a church structure, but you're dead. You have money in the bank, but you're dead. You have a slamming choir but you're still dead. You have a charismatic and suave homilitition in the pulpit, but you're still dead. In a sense the risen Lord says, *"I'm not like men. I can see through you and you are really dead"*! He tells Sardis that they are dead. The pulsating heartbeat that they once had for community organization and development had been arrested by their apathy of what was going on in the very neighborhood that they were situated in… their dead. The cancer of assimilation and accommodation moved throughout their organizational body as they refuse the chemotherapy of dignity and African identity…their dead. The homicidal maniac of bad theology as it relates to prosperity had stalked them and had murdered their ability to care for the least of these… their dead. Yet while their great big church had a sign on the marque that said Living A.M.E.Zion church, the risen Lord subtly suggests that underneath the name of the church they ought to write an epithet which says, *"Ashes to ashes, and dust to dust"*. While people believed that the church was alive, the Lords analysis was that they were really dead. When the church at Sardis heard this they were heartbroken. They were crushed. They were discouraged. They were embarrassed. They felt low. Yet the risen Lord says to them, *"don't forget how you feel after receiving this word"*.

The risen Lord was quite aware that if they remembered how they felt inwardly, they would be more careful about what they did outwardly. When I was a little boy, I was riding my big wheel in the basement. As I was riding I noticed this thing in the wall that had two slits and a hole. Being an inquisitive child I went up to it and put a paper clip in the hole. The bright flash and the burning sensation caused me to get my little behind back on the big wheel and fly out of there with lightning speed! Whenever I have to do something electrical, (plug something in, put on jumper cables ect)) I always get an irksome fear because I remembered how I felt when I did the wrong thing. The risen Lord says don't forget how you feel right now as your receiving this word.

The good news is that he provides them with the tools of being a living church. The fact is that the risen Lord cannot use a dead church. A dead church has never been the propellant for effective church growth. A lifeless church has never been the springboard for transformational communities of faith. A deceased church is always a decreasing church. Ministry becomes misery, preaching becomes impotent, and worship becomes routine when the church is dead. The good news here is that in the midst of this diagnosis of death, the risen Lord provides *direction* for a *resurrection*. His words of discipline are always coupled with the way of discipleship. The steps of making a move from a fronting church to a God satisfied ministry are in the text. It begins with looking out. It is amazing how the risen Lord uses a historical context to give a spiritual warning. The message of the risen Lord reflects upon a time when the Sardians felt that the city was impenetrable. It was located in a rather mountainous region, which was difficult to ascend and conquer. Cyrus had his eye on Sardis and told his soldiers to keep their eyes on Sardis. The word on the block was that any man who could find a way to penetrate Sardis would receive a special reward. Hyeroeades gazed relentlessly at the city on a cliff when he saw a Sardian soldier drop his helmet down the backside of the mountain. Not thinking, the soldier retrieved the helmet and ascended the mount. Cyrus's soldiers quietly followed the Lydian soldier and took the city. It is out of this context that the risen Lord encourages the Sardians to protectively watch. The poor Sardian soldier didn't watch out for the watchers. One act made the city completely vulnerable. An effective pastor has to know what to look out for as it relates to the protection of the membership. He or she can never cajole ideas or practices that are destructive to the message and the ministry of the Kingdom. He or she can never be a political participant in the dysfunctional downfall of the church. The directive is to watch! Effective pastors watch out for worldly philosophical approaches, bad theology, and cultural immorality, which watches intently to invade the churches fortress. One interpretation of this word "watch" means to wake up!! Effective pastors work to prevent the congregation from being lulled into a dogmatic slumber by the lack of study. They are active in preventing the congregation from the drowsiness of meaningless liturgies, pointless sermons, and worthless teaching. The risen Lord says, "*watch*"! Effective pastors are always more engaged with watching out for the membership as oppose to looking out for self. Effective church leadership becomes productive, when the congregations can effectively distinguish between leaders who are in it because they have been called and leaders who are in it because they have costs. It is worth noting also that effective pastors (according to this passage) are not the only watchers among the membership. As effective pastors receive from God, the effective pastor gives vision to others in the membership. Effective watchers teach others to watch. Although I am convinced that certain sermons should be ongoing, I do believe that every pastor at some point ought to look at what is happening in contemporary culture and do a series of sermons entitled, "what the church must look out for". Watchers should be on the trustee board. Watchers should be on the steward board. Watchers should be in the lay council. Watchers should be in Christian education. The risen Lord calls us to watch! Well we discover that the text is tailored to teach us that we must look out, but the text teaches us that we must look in. The Lord is no longer speaking to the members that are putting up a front. The risen Lord moves from the fake to the for real. He is speaking to the ones who have not soiled their garments. The risen Lord gives a clarion call for an introspection, which leads to strengthening the things that remain and are dying. It is a call for Sardis to look inside of itself and give strength to things that are on the critical list within the membership. It is the miraculous move to take the dying stuff off life support and get it back in the life cycle. Jesus says, *"Look at yourself and strengthen that which remains, but is dying"*. The risen Lord purposefully is not definitive about what the dying things are, because quite frankly it's no one else's business. Misrepresentations and misinterpretations were at the heart of the problem. Many pundits and prognosticators had already concluded that Sardis church was the spot. They had it going on. However the risen Lord who knew what was really going on in the church said that the world thinks you're alive, but I know your dead. *"Those things"* which he references are between the

Lord and the church. The risen Lord is not going to splatter their business all over the empire. It is between the church and the Lord. The risen Lord provides them with a metaphor for rescuing the dying. He says to bring stability to the things that are dying. As I looked at the theological interpretation and etymological breakdown of this passage, I was rather drawn to an imaginative picturesque model of what *strengthening those things which remain but that are dying* looks like. My mind was taken to the aftermath of a bloody battle. The stench of gunfire fills the air as the smoke hovers above the ground like dancing ghosts of what use to be. The field is covered with the bodies of fervent warriors who have paid the ultimate price of passion for their patriotism. As they lay lifeless on the ground, with helmet cocked halfway off their head, the weapons of their warfare lay in tribute next to them. Yet on the field of death, a breath is heard… A gasp, a cry for help. For while death is all around, there is a soldier that remains. A spirit teetering on the brink and brim of death is happy as a medic comes, gives strength, and snatches him from the jaws of death. At this point it must be noted that ministry leaves many casualties. The pastor who has left the ministry because of church politics is a casualty. The congregation, which is split due to a handful of devils, is a casualty. The first lady who chooses to place her membership at another church is a casualty. The children who struggle with the hypocrisy of some members are casualties of the church. Yet we discover that the risen Lord is dependent on we who have strength to give strength. The bowed head of a discouraged pastor is to be lifted by we who have strength. The broken heart which manifests itself in a broken body is to be mended back together again by we who have strength. The shattered pieces of disassembled families in ministry are called to be reassembled by we who have strength. The bible study on Tuesday who only has 2 or 3, the Sunday school class that only has 1, the financial resources that have dried up, are all called to be attended to by we who have strength. For it is in the context of this text that the risen Lord is dependent upon us to....

Lift him up....lift him up.....till he speaks from eternity......and if I if I be lifted up from the earth I'll draw all men unto me!!

CHAPTER 6

And No Man Can Shut It

Behold I have set before thee an open door,
and no man can shut it. Revelation 3:8

As I contemplated the thematic emphasis of this text and sought to discover from it a single sermonic title, I found that the title is f within the 6 words of the passage. The text says, *"and no man can shut it"*. What is most significant however is the imagery of this open door, and more significant is the one who is holding the door open. We discover here that the text teaches us theological implications of the Lords authority *over* the church, the Lords power *in* the church and the Lords support *of* the church. He has the authority; the power and the ability to hold the door open for the church at Philadelphia. Is there a true shepherd that in the midst of his or her pastoral struggles pleads for an open door?

Locked into the minutia of meaningless traditions, tempers

rising from the clandestine cabin fever of the same ole same ole, inwardly oppressed by the stress that comes from the demands of pastoring a local church, a district, or an annual conference is there a true shepherd that doesn't want an open door? In a very real sense the open door is reflective of an open opportunity. It represents another chance. Jesus says, "*I will open a door that no man can shut*". Biblical scholarship notes the geography and the essential purpose of "Philly". It was situated on the boarders of Mysia, Lydia and Phrygia. Its purpose was to spread Greek culture and language.

It was an evangelical tool of Greek culture and ideas. It was afforded an opportunity to be in a position to do the missionary work of culture building. So effective was its work that there were some cities who forgot their entire language and spoke the Greek dialect exclusively. Maysia, Lydia, and Phrygia represented an opportunity for Philadelphia. It was an open door. In the text Jesus is speaking to the church. He says, "*because you have maintained a little strength, because you have kept my word, because you have not denied my name, because you have maintained your integrity in the worst of circumstances, because you have not swayed to please and appease the polls of popular opinion,, I have set before you an opportunity.*

What is the psychological approach and the emotional stance of the Philadelphia angel as he/she stands before the open door? I have been at many annual conferences where the Episcopate calls the name of the newly appointed pastor and the pastor takes his or her time getting up because they don't know what's on the other side of the open door. I know many pastors who when they have been asked to go back to the appointment, they wonder whether they want to put up with the foolishness for another 12 months, 365 days, 1440 minuets.. they are ambiguous at the open door. In a sense it was a given opportunity to work unaware of the dangers, toils, and snares of the field. It was a chance to work amidst the pain of the wilderness but the joy of the promise land. It was an opportunity to experience the joy of Jericho victory, but the loss of Ziglag. It was an opportunity to experience the pain of Calvary but the Joy of resurrection morning. Jesus said I have set before you an open door. How does one approach the open door? How do I deal with the given opportunity given not necessarily by the Bishop, but by God? Do we feel the urgency and the unction to do a great work or are we apprehensive and afraid to get involved? Do we have what it takes or will it take what we have? What is our reaction to the open door? The nature of the reaction ought to be based upon the hermeneutical and exegetical analysis of this apocalyptic text. We discover primarily that the anointed one has all authority to appoint. The personal pronoun of this exclamitive sentence is specific. Jesus says *"I"* have set before thee an open door. Not the Episcopate, not the search committee, not the pulpit committee. Jesus says "I". The text is teaching us that there is a composite of dust and divinity in the appointing process, which represents the dust of the Episcopate, and the divinity of God.

Is it possible that we suffer delusions of grandeur believing that the sole source of the appointing process is man? Do we fail to understand that the appointer who gives the appointment is through the anointed? Nothing happens beyond the sovereignty of God. The text adequately presents the vicar as the mere vessel in the overall purpose and plan of God.. In the tradition of the AME Zion church, we base our going hither and thither on the Godly judgment of the Bishop. Is it possible that we should rather choose to trust the personal conformation of the anointed through the vessel? . Jesus said, "*I have set before you*". The personal pronoun of this passage is progressive. It is one, which I can hinge my hopes and my aspirations upon. It is one upon which I can move fearlessly through a nonproductive pastorate.

Through this personal pronoun, I can walk through the open door knowing with confidence that no weapon that is formed against me shall prosper. Through this personal pronoun, I can trust that thousands may fall around me, but it shall not come nigh to me. That pronoun shows up through out the New Testament. When congregational drama leaves you spiritually famished and starving, he says, "*I am the bread of life*". When the shepherd becomes a sheep and is in need of a green pastures and still waters, when no one is there to shepherd the shepherd, he says, "*I am the good shepherd, the good shepherd gives his life for the sheep*". When the good pastor is surrounded by death... dead choir members, dead trustees, dead stewards, dead deacons, dead presiding Elders, dead Bishops, he says, "*I am the resurrection and the life. He that believeth in me though he were dead yet shall he live*". The temptation to get it twisted is ever present. He is the one who ultimately gives the appointment., and whatever the nature of the appointment is, if you have a connection with the anointed advocate ....like Gloria Gaynor, you will survive.

There is something else that is intriguing about this text. I have.... *"set"* before you an open door. The passage reflects the setting of a setup. The key to unlocking this profound proclamation from the prince of peace is in the word "set". One interpretation says, *"I have given you something that works to your advantage"*. We stand before the door not knowing what awaits us on the other side. We are ambiguous about what hasn't happened but what could happen. We are emotionally shell shocked over worst-case scenarios reminiscent of bad past experiences. Yet the risen Lord reminds us that where I am putting you is a pilgrimage of faith Your view may be confined to the local drama of tricky trustees. Your view may be confined to the local view of silly stewards or precarious preachers. Your view may be confined to lack of assessment for annual conference just 2 weeks away. In all of this you may not find any purpose in ministry or reason for being. However Jesus says I have given you a situation that is advantageous to you. I have put you in a place that may not help you in the right now, but it will be advantageous to you in the future. I have *"set"* before you!

In the sitcom *"a different world"*, Kimberly Reece's father has been shot. In the midst of the crisis, her friends are with here in the hospital. It seems that Freddy prays and asks God to heal Kim's dad but he gets worse. She becomes frustrated in her faith, because she can't understand why God just doesn't give us what we want. Dwayne Wayne gives the most profound illustration. He tells the story of how one year for Christmas he wanted a truck, a basketball and a few other items. With child like anxiety and boundless excitement he couldn't wait for Christmas to come. Everyday brought him closer to exploding with joy and happiness. When Christmas came he realized that there were some things he didn't get. He didn't get a truck, but he got a jacket. He didn't get a basketball, but he got some gloves. Obviously he was a little disappointed. However, the next week there was a major snowstorm, and he discovered, he couldn't put a truck on his back to stay warm. He couldn't put a basketball on his hands to keep them snug. He discovered that what he got was what he really needed.

Yes!!! You may be pastoring a church that other preachers have run from. Yes!! They may not understand worship through the flow of the anointing. Yes!! They may be a poor church with no money in the bank. The good news is that God has put you there now, because God is shaping you for your destiny tomorrow. God is using bad experiences to shape you, tears at night to make you, faith to recreate you and hope to take you. And so our prayer should be the prayer of the songwriter... *Have thine own way Lord.... Have thine own way.... Thou art the potter...I am the clay...Mold me and make me after thine will, while I am yielded perfect and still.*

CHAPTER 7

An Exchange For Change

We arrive at church this Sunday morning and there is a sense of discouragement in the atmosphere. Ex –cathedra the pastor sits in the chair, with his head hung low. The musicians have left, the praise team has been seated, the ministers surround the Pastor and the church doors have been closed. There is a sense of resignation and hopelessness in the air. Upon some faces the tears, which arise from the cumulous clouds of the soul, pour from the unlevied eyes. Sniffles can be heard from the mothers' board. Handkerchiefs are taken out from the pockets of the deacon board, and the silent cry is "*by the rivers of Babylon we wept when we thought about Zion*". Some contemplate leaving while others wonder if its worth staying. What has caused this woeful and sorrowful scenario?

The Church at Laodicea had a very interesting social context. She was a church that was situated amidst a city that was prospering. The city was in a historical season of great prosperity. It was a city, which was a major financial center throughout the entire empire. She was a renowned financial lending institution. It is said that Cicero did much of his banking in Laodicea. When an earthquake devastated the city, the empire offered to help her rebuild. Laodicea however refused the help because she was financially stable enough to rebuild it herself. Imagine the victims of Katrina saying to the federal Government, " *We don't want your help, we're going to rebuild it ourselves*". (Somewhere in this there is a lesson about Black Nationalism and economic development).

She was not only financially renowned; she was also a textile giant. She was known for her product of black shiny wool. It was a hot item among Laodicea's hoy paloy. She was not only known for her financial prosperity, she was not only known for her textiles, she was known as one of the best medical centers through out all of Asia minor. Her specialty was ophthalmology. She was known to have possessed eye salve that healed the eyes. Ritenbaugh suggest that she had one problem. Most prosperous cities were built around water. Laodicea had no water resources around her. Water had to be piped in from about 9 miles. From Collose, she received cold water, and from Hierapolis she received hot water. However when the water arrived in Laodicea it was sickeningly lukewarm. The city had a problem amidst their prosperity. If they were attacked from a raiding army, and the water supply was cut off, she would have suffered massive casualties. In a sense she was at the mercy of the empire for the most basic thing which sustains life…. water. This was the problem in the city.

The problem in the church was worst. The church suffered a problem, which swung between the pendulums of illusion and disillusion. They had an illusory self-image. They were the big church on the district and in the big city. They enjoyed the casual relationship with those who were significant in the city at large. Money poured in from affluent tithers. In the contextual analysis of how the world at large defined success, they had it goin on like neck bones.

There self-analysis and self evaluation caused them to conclude with a three fold illusion. They said, "*I am rich, I don't need anything, and I am increased in goods*". The mission statement on the marquis of the church read, "*I am rich, I am increased with Goods, and I don' need anything*". . Indelibly inscribed in the bulletin were the words, "*I am rich I am incased in goods and don't need anything*". The business cards that were handed out by the Pastor read, "*I am rich, increased in goods and I don't need anything*". That made them feels like somebody in the judgments and estimating eyes of the world around them. That was the epitome of their value system regarding ministry. That was their illusion. However they failed to realize that the risen Lord had a different context and construct which in the end left them as they truly were…. wretched, miserable, poor, blind, and naked. The definition of what true success was had flipped. They failed to realize that the estimation of who you are in the eyes of the world means nothing in comparison to who you are in the eyes of God. What the world says is different from what God says. In the eyes of men they were settled. In the eyes of God they were jacked up. In the eyes of man they had stability and lacked nothing. In the eyes of God they were naked and poor.

What matters most is not what others say about you. What matters is how God sees you. When the illusion is destroyed, the disillusion kicks in. One becomes disillusioned and depressed because what they thought was a feather in their cap became an arrow in their flesh. At this level one has to establish a whole different context and adapt to the true context. Jesus told them who they really were. And so... We arrive at church this Sunday morning and there is a sense of discouragement and disappointment in the atmosphere. Ex –cathedra the pastor sits in the chair, with his head hung low. The musicians have left, the praise team has been seated, the ministers surround the pastor and the church doors have been closed. There is a sense of resignation and hopelessness in the air. Upon some faces, the tears, which arise from the cumulous clouds of the soul, pour from the unlevied eyes. Sniffles can be heard from the mothers' board. Handkerchiefs are taken out from the pockets of the deacon board, and the silent cry is "by the rivers of Babylon we wept when we thought about Zion". Some contemplate leaving while others wonder if it's worth staying.

What has caused this woeful and sorrowful scenario? It is the letter that Pastor has received from the Bishop of our souls. They are disillusioned and disheartened. However as Pastor reads further, the pastors' head snaps back up!! He shouts, " *wait a minuet.... there is hope*"! It is in an exchange that brings the possibility of change! The congregation lifts its head as Pastor reads on. Known for being a financially prosperous city, the risen Lord becomes their financial advisor. He encourages them to Invest in gold tried by the fire. All hope is not lost because the risen Lord still sees something that they posses. They are not bankrupt. He says, "*buy*". The balanced perspective of the risen Lord dares to suggest that they are economically viable in the marketplace of exchange. They are poor, but not that poor. They still have a few coins in their pockets. Even in the worst church the risen Lord sees potential. The pastor who is amidst a fire trying pastorate, the Pastor who has a laundry list of faults and failures regarding the hostile experience, and the pastor who scarcely sees any good in the appointment must search for the good in the ministry no matter how concealed and hidden it may be. The risen Lord didn't want to crush them into resignation, he wanted to prompt and push them using the little they had…buying power! The first call to change the risen Lord makes is a clarion call to Invest. He says, "*Buy gold tried by the fire*". Gold tried in the fire is metaphorical for that which has lost the dross of foolishness and pettiness in order to get at that which is real and valuable. One of the practices that the pastor must become involved with is learning not to get caught up in the dross. One cannot afford to get caught up in the mess of the drossites. The drossites will take all of the attention off that which is real and authentic. Drossites hijack worship experiences sand create a negative cloud above the head of the entire church.

Drossites tempt the preacher to spend too much time battling the foolishness as oppose to preaching what's real. Drossites bring the foolishness to trustee board meeting, steward board meetings and to members meeting as well. God is not interested in the dross, he is looking for Laodicea to invest in that, which is real. Drossites cause the preacher to be the catalyst for the disease of negativity in te congregation. The preaching becomes so negative that many are unfed when it comes to life sustaining truths. Jesus says, "*buy from me gold where the dross has been burned away.*" The ultimate goal of all pastoring is to develop a 24-carrot spirituality that is unshakeable. The purpose of all preaching is the presentation of that which is real and that which is true. In the end we are called to live that which is real, true, and has value in the eyes of God. Jesus gives a call to invest. The clarion call is not only to invest in gold tried by the fire; it is a call for investment in adequate attire.

I do not participate in symbolism draped in color cultural bias. To me the color of the linen or clothes is irrelevant. Laodecians thought they were dressed to the "t" but in the eyes of God they were streaking. The term streaking is a 70's term that was definitive of people who would run up to you with no clothes on and run off. Imagine being on a beautiful date in the park, holding hands and looking lovingly into each other's eyes, when all of a sudden a naked man jumps out of the bushes turkey naked! They lacked the clothing of care and compassion. They lacked the clothing of morality. They lacked the clothing of justice in the courts, fairness in employment, and equality in education. They were proud to be streaking in the front of God. Big budgets don't compensate for being a streaker in Gods eyes. Having plush economic resources don't compensate for nasty nudity before God. Fame and notoriety doesn't compensate for being a spiritual streaker. God expects the pastor to be adequately dressed. The Bible says that we are to put on the whole armor of God. The risen Lord not only calls Laodicea to invest in gold tried by the fire, he not only calls them to invest in adequate attire, but he calls them to invest in eye salve. We have earlier mentioned that Laodicea was known for their healing eye salve. The claim was that it could heal anything that affected ones vision. It would affect how the person would see things. In a sense Jesus says, "*buy spiritual eye salve from me so that you can see and understand life better*". I went through one of the most hair-raising events in my life.

The doctor told me that there were to many blood vessels growing behind my retina. He said that he was going to have to give me a needle in my eye. Immediately I thought it would be a needle that would come out of the back of my head. I discovered that it was a little needle. At any rate, when they gave me the medicine my vision went completely dark. God knows I love My Cherie Amour by Stevie Wonder, but I didn't want to be blind. After a while my vision slowly came back brighter than ever. Many pastors need spiritual eye salve to see things with new and fresh perspectives. We often can be in a bad situation… so bad that spiritually our vision becomes clouded and we cant see our way. I challenge every pastor to buy the eye salve from God. Buy the salve of prayer so that you can have a fresh look. Buy the eye salve of faith so that you will be confident knowing that God has your past, your present and your future in the palm of his hand. Buy the eye salve of praise so that you can really see what to shout about. I guess I love the church at Laodicea because of the tender way the letter closes the pronouncement. With heeds hung low, with a spirit of resignation, as they walk away in hopelessness, Jesus shouts "*Laodicea!!... I love you*"!!! That is enough to make anyone to want to straighten up and fly right!!!

CHAPTER 8

Passing Through, Coming To, And Continuing On

But he passing through the midst of them
went he his way. And he came down to
Capernaum, a city of Galilee and taught
them in their synagogue. Luke 4;30-31

As I write this chapter I do so with painful reflection. For in doing so I reflect upon the many pastors that have not been afforded the opportunity to have positive pastoral experiences. Ministry for me ain't been no crystal stare or no flowery bed of ease. There have been highs, and there have been lows. There have been moments of satisfaction and there have been moments of sore disappointment. The commitment to conveying truth has cost me much. I am among the few who have been thrown out of a church. It was not because I was caught stealing money. It was not because I had substance abuse issues. It was not because I was a church whore. It was because of my commitment to convey truth. Pastoral decisions had to be made in order that the life of the church would move on. I had to make certain decisions in order that the church wouldn't fizzle away and limp on its last legs to a dismal and abysmal future.

In each scenario, the church needed an attractive worship experience. However because the people were to cheap to build a viable music ministry, even when dynamic musicians, (many from C.O.G.I.C or the Apostolic church) came to take us higher in worship, to retaliate, they would sit like croaking frogs on a log grieving and quenching the spirit of God. In each scenario the church needed to do community evangelism. However, because of a family church orientation, the ministry of the church exclusively evolved around big mamma, auntie and uncle, as no one else in the surrounding community mattered. In each scenario the church was in need of Christian education. However a handful would come out to bible study and Sunday school. In the end there was a clashing of ministry values between pastor and people. When that happens, not much work can be done. Although I was chased out from a church, the reasons were very similar. Members of the official boards, along with other tag alongs had problems with change.

They did not have the spiritual eyes to see that certain moves and decisions had to be made in order that the life of the church would move on. At any rate, connectional pastors know the drill. Members work the Presiding Elder, the Elder works the Bishop and the Bishop lifts the appointment. In the end, a family who had made many investments in the church is thrown out on the street. A psychotherapist would have a field day with diagnosing the psychological stability of a pastor who's been kicked out of the church. When it happened to me, I wanted nothing to do with God, church, or family. All of them could kiss my...well you know.. However after a while I learned that being thrown out for the right reason was a good thing, and that I was in good company with this experience. In the context of this text we discover that Jesus came to the synagogue. It was his custom to participate in the worship experience by reading the scripture and exegeting the text. The text was read so beautifully as this homeboy and son of the community caught the pensive look of the congregants. He spoke as one who had authority. But then as the sermon moved on, something happened. John Hemer talks about the anti climactic nature of the sermon. To people who expected the fulfillment of this text to come by way of a bloody revolution, Jesus says, "*today this text has been fulfilled in your hearing*". Furthermore in a sense he says, "*You think God exclusively belongs to you. However the fact is God also loves the one you hate, and cherishes the one that you think your better than. The brother whose pants are saggin...God loves him. The sister who got all them kids...God loves them. The individual that sleeps in a cardboard box...God loves them. The one who isn't in your bougie neighborhood, the one who is straight out the hood, God loves them*". When they heard this, they were enraged. They put him out of the synagogue, brought him to a cliff and tried to throw him off. Evans notes that they wanted to stone him.

He notes that in that day there were two types of stoning. The one that was reserved for Jesus was such that after they threw him over the cliff, they would then crush him with a huge rock. Jesus however escaped safely. Yet the sad part of the narrative is that he was thrown out. The primary lesson here to neophyte pastors is that upon entering a pastorate it is possible that the membership will not receive what you have to offer.

Wickedness may plug their ears, ignorance may blind their eyes, and selfishness may block their heart. It is possible that after all the labor, after all the midnight tears, after all the sacrifice and after all of the praying, they may still throw you out. As a footnote to all of this let me suggest that it is not just the pastor that they throw out. They also throw out the family. The spouse is chased away from employment, and the children are chased away from their schooling. The positive image of God and church are cynically shaped into a negative ideology. They are thrown out. I recall the pain of being thrown out of this particular church. In spite of the formula for success that my father had instilled in me, I was thrown out.

The drudgery of packing up an entire house that I believed I would retire from weighed heavily on my spirit. The disgust that my wife had on her face, and the stained mark of distrust that she has in her spirit regarding church people, The look of misunderstanding that the children had on their face as they ask the question, "*daddy why do we have to move*"?, weighed on me heavily. To this day I struggle to forgive the Bishop, who listened to the Elder who was won by devils in the church. When the last box was packed, as I was about to walk through the kitchen doorway, I looked over my shoulder at what I was leaving and collapsed in tears. One decision caused me to close my ears to the comfort of the Holy Ghost. One decision caused me to turn my back on my family. One decision caused me to almost have an adulterous affair on my wife. I went through all of this because I didn't have a clue on how to handle being thrown out by tricky trustees, silly stewards and critical congregants. I am at a point now where in peace I can reflectively ask myself what have I learned. How did Jesus handle it?

What was the approach of Jesus? First of all, it says he *passed through them*. He would not stay and try to win them over. He would not stay and try to bring the congregation together. At this point the solution was not to be negotiable diplomatic or uniting. He passed through. It is certainly ironic that if Jesus pastored a church today, the directive would be to love the people, and gain the congregations trust. The counsel would have been to win them over to your side. This naive directive negates the fact that when the mindset of a congregation is maniacle, there is no negotiating. There is no diplomacy. There is no cajoling.

Sometimes you have to just pass straight through them. The potential of loosing oneself and ones ministry is greater when the leader doesn't let go, and pass through untouched on to the next assignment. Through the text we discover that where a church wants to place you has nothing to do with where God wants to take you. Sometimes where God wants to take you can only be accomplished by where the Lord has placed you. The congregation grabbed a hold of him. The word for "thrust" in the text means to violently push. They violently pushed him out of the pulpit. They were impressed by the way he stood with authority before them. However as he began to preach, they went into flip mode. Smiling faces turned to flagrant frowns. The glee and glisten in their eye turned dismal and dark. "Who is this" changed to " "Who does he think he is"? One ran up to the pulpit…. then two… then three. In a moment the whole congregation was in an uproar, throwing this fearless dark child out on the street.

The calm streets of Nazareth were disturbed. People joined the motley crowd as they pushed and shoved him. In the end, they became so violent and rambunctious that they lost track of him. The text says that he was able to pass through without being hurt. There are just so many lessons in this part of the passage that it would consume the entire book. One could easily look at the fact that he didn't allow any one to detour his destiny. He allowed no one to get a hold on him. One of the biggest challenges that pastors face in rebellious congregations is fighting to keep the congregation from figuratively putting their hands on them and taking pastors to a destructive destiny. Pastors become combative, frustrated, depressed, and discouraged because they have allowed misled, misguided, and misinformed members to put their hands on them and take them to a destructive destiny. Some times the answer isn't to go toe to toe with them; sometimes the answer is to just get away from them.

Sometimes the answer is to recognize early what they want to do with you and then just pass through. The larger lesson here is that not all pastorates are meant to be lengthy. Some pastorates are just meant to be weighing stations for a different destiny. Jesus just passed through. Consider the crowd. They were obstinate, they had problems with receiving truth, they were violent, and they wanted to terminate his ministry. Jesus was no fool, and I'm convinced that he doesn't want us to be a fool either. There are certain questions that we need to ask ourselves when we find ourselves in these particular situations. First of all, "based on their past and their present will they ever really get it"? More than likely the personality of this congregation had been this way for a long time. This was no sporadic situation that occurred out of osmosis. It may have been that the goodness of Jesus ignited the gritty wickedness that was deep in the heart of the members. With all of my preaching, with all of my teaching, with all of the workshops and seminars will they ever really get it?

Is it really worth the effort and energy? Knowing that time is not promised to any of us and aware that time is filled with swift transition is it really worth staying among people who are trying to remove you? I remember driving with one of our aluminous Bishops. He shared with me," *Ed, if a church has made no change in 4 years, if they have not grown spiritually or numerically in four years, it may be time to leave*". Bishop Clarence Car use to remind the preachers at annual conference that a Bishop never had to remove an appointment from him. He always knew when his tenure was up. The water gets murkier. Sometimes a pastor genuinely believes that he can turn the church around. In his heart he or she believes that if they work hard enough the church may do what the church is called to do. Many Pastors fail to realize that there are some Churches that God allows us to go to just to pass through. I have found that God uses some pastors to give congregations another chance to turn around. However when its time to go its time to go. We must never forget that Jesus was an itinerate preacher. I'll never forget that at one church, God was telling me clearly that it was time to go. However I believed that I could turn the church around. In fact the church was really doing well. However God said it was time to go. I did more ministry, worked longer hours, and increased my counseling schedule, but God said it was time to go. The late R.D. Henton told me its time to go! I went to hear Evangelist Jackie McCullough preach and the title of her sermon was prepare to be ejected. One day while taking a breather and looking out the front window, God caused a huge mayflower moving truck to park right in front of my house. God was saying its time to go!

The other question is do they share bible centered ministry values. What is in their past? Is it reflective of a congregation that shares bible values? Is their present status reflective of members who share common bible values? What has been the emphasis in the past five years? These are just few questions that help you to understand whether this is a stable appointment or whether it is a passing through appointment. I dare not overwork the point. There are times when God appoints you to a post because he wants you to learn something. Often Pastoral learning doesn't come from a flagship appointment. Often good solid pastoral learning doesn't come from a seminary. Sometimes God puts a pastor in a position so that he or she can learn.

There were some things that I learned in the pastorate that I didn't learn in the seminary. There were lessons that I had to learn in tears that I couldn't learn in the classroom. A pastor must never forget that when it seems like nothing is working out, when the battles seem to be many and the victories seem to be few, when the spirit grows weary of praying, God is trying to teach you something. Jesus simply passed through. However we note something else here. Jesus not only passed through, but *he went to.* What meanest thou good doctor? He didn't allow the bad experience of a previous pastorate to prevent him from moving forward in ministry. The text says that he went down to Capernaum. Herin is the fatal mistake I made in that particular season of my ministry. When my appointment had been lifted, I had become so devastated that it took me about three years to get back in the swing again.

My world fell apart and I wanted nothing to do with church. I found myself waddling in the puddles of pain. I had to share with someone. I really needed counseling, but people were either tired of hearing my whining, or they just plain didn't want to be bothered. Its like a man with broken legs being told to get up and in spite of his efforts, he falls back down. There are some that you expect to have the tools to help you get yourself together only to discover that they have no tools at all. There are those who do have the tools who when you talk, its like talking a foreign language. I became my own barrier. At this juncture of my life I am learning that even when you have been hurt, you still have to move. I imagine that Jesus could have cried (and he probably did) I imagine that he could have complained. I imagine he could have been angry. I imagine that he could have apathetically sent them all to hell. However the bible says in spite of all of the rejection, in spite of all of the anger, in spite of all of the violence, He kept it moving. I believe that he focused on his purpose. His over all-purpose was greater than some little Nazareth church that didn't want to go anywhere. Purpose should keep you moving. Yes, they wrote a letter to the Bishop. Yes, the Presiding Elder is running interference in your pastorate. Yes, there are devils in the church that are organizing to kick you and your family out on the street. Yes, your appointment is unfairly one year at a time. Yes, you've been embarrassed at the annual conference. However your overall purpose is greater than trivial foolishness. Members in a congregation may have no desire to receive the word. They may have no desire to engage in meaningful ministry. They may just want to fight. However your overall purpose is bigger than this. At this particular church, as the congregation was organizing to throw me out, as they were threatening the Bishop that if he didn't remove me they would close up their pocketbooks, As I traveled 2 hours to them after a nine to five Job, after they cut my salary so much that I had no gas money to get to them, As their wicked selves could bow with pseudo sincerity at the altar of God, and plot and scheme devilish deeds...I kept on visiting my sick and shut in.

I kept on walking through the nursing home with patients puling on my clothes asking for prayer. I laid hands on them.

I kept driving an hour and a half with bad eyes in the dark to bible study, where none of the devils showed up, but only a handful of the faithful. I kept it moving. The internalization of pastoral mobility is significantly important. If it means keeping it moving to another appointment, keep it moving. If it means moving to a different denomination, keep it moving. If it means moving out of state, or even out of the country, keep it moving. We learn from the text that Jesus not only passed through, he not only went to, but he continued on. In other words he realized that in spite of it all, the work had to go on.

On the road of pastoral ministry the streets are littered with the fallen carcasses of pastors who have painfully declared," *It is enough, I quit"*. Consider the statistics from Pastoral Care Inc. *From our recent research we did to retest our data, 1050 pastors were surveyed Five hundred ninety, (590 or 57%) said they would leave if they had a better place to go- including secular work. Eighty- one percent (81%) of polled pastors said there was no regular discipleship program or effective effort of mentoring their people or teaching them to deepen their Christian formation at their church (remember these are the Reformed and Evangelical- not the mainline pastors!). (This is Key) Eight hundred eight (808 or 77%) of the pastors we surveyed felt they did not have a good marriage! Seven hundred ninety (790 or 75%) of the pastors we surveyed felt they were unqualified and/or poorly trained by their seminaries to lead and manage the church or to counsel others. This left them disheartened in their ability to pastor. Seven hundred fifty-six (756 or 72%) of the pastors we surveyed stated that they only studied the Bible when they were preparing for sermons or lessons. This left only 38% who read the Bible for devotions and personal study. Three hundred ninety-nine (399 or 38%) of pastors said they were divorced or in a divorce process Three hundred fifteen (315 or 30%) said they had Two hundred seventy (270 or 26%) of pastors said they regularly had personal devotions and felt they were adequately fed spirituality. (This is Key). Two hundred forty-one (241 or 23%) of the pastors surveyed said they felt happy and content on a regular basis with who they are in Christ, in their church, and in their home! Of the pastors surveyed, they stated that a mean (average) of only 25% of their church's membership attended a Bible Study or small group at least twice a month.*

All of this is enough to make a pastor quit. There were events in the ministry of Jesus that could have made him quit. He was thrown out of Nazareth church. He was told to leave a city even after he healed a man from demon possession. There were countless Pharisees, and Sadducees who followed him to try to make a fool out of him. A court of slicker's and thugs falsely accused him. He was beat down by the Roman pretoriate. His disciples deserted him. He was nailed to a cross in the front of his mother. Much could have made him say I quit. He didn't quit because mission out weighed misery. He didn't quit because Disappointment became Gods appointment. He didn't quit because tears turned to triumph. He didn't quit. And so like Paul we boldly hunger to say with authority... " *I am now ready to be offered and my departure is at hand. I have fought a good fight".*

CHAPTER 9

Every Sunday Palm Sunday

And the crowds that went before him and that
followed him were shouting "Hosanna to the son of
David, Blessed is he who comes in the name of the
Lord. Hosanna to the highest." Mathew 21:8-10

A young man entered the church one Sunday morning.
As he stood in the foyer of the church, he noticed that
there was an assemblage of names with a little flag next to the
name. He wondered what it could mean. As the pastor took
notice of this puzzled child he walked up and stood next to him.
The young child asked," *pastor, what do those names mean*"?
"*Well*" the pastor retorted, "*Those are the names of men and
women who died in the service*". The little boy looked back up
at the names and asked, "*The 9:30 service or the 11:00 service*"?
No preacher enjoys being a part of a dead worship experience.
I gather that the reason for this is because dead worship is a

cancer that consumes everyone in reach. The autopsy report of a dead worship experience is singularly familiar. It begins with an *ambiguous attitude about worship*. I have always felt that certain periods of history have done a good job of destroying true worship.

In the estimation of some historical periods, any worship that was overtly expressive and too emotional was determined to be unsophisticated and barbaric to say the least. The autopsy of Dead worship not only reveals the evidence of ambiguity about worship, it reveals *the anemia in the practice of worship*. I have been in worship experience where the fire could be burning in one section of the church, but dying out (or not even be ignited) in another part of the church. There is no continuity in the practice of raising ones hand, saying amen, speaking in lounges, or doing the holy dance. Some are content to just sit and observe. Well we discover that there is not only ambiguity about worship, there is not only anemia regarding the practice of worship, there is *apathy in the presence of worship*. God wakes us up every morning. Daily God feeds our family. Daily God gives us a Job to go to.

Daily God protects us and blesses us. Yet in the worship experience some have become so apathetic, that in the words of Shakespeare, worship is much ado about nothing. A dead worship experience is always counterproductive to the practice of evangelism. Evangelism seeks to draw people in; dead worship tends to push people out. For every member that evangelism brings in, a dead church will push them further away from the things of God. A sane pastor hungers for a Palm Sunday worship experience. Good worship enlarges the boundaries of hope. Good worship brings encouragement to the brokenness of the spirit. Good worship breaks the bonds of congregational exclusivity.

Every sane pastor hungers for the Palm Sunday experience. In the practical expressions of theology manifested in what is called the worship service, there has never been a time when I didn't need good worship. I have preached in many academic circles and have preached across denominational lines. I have preached at big boring churches and mid-size fire baptized churches. Yet in spite of it all I have never been in a situation where sitting in the pulpit I didn't desire for the Holy Ghost to come and set the place a blaze. Every pastor ought to hunger for the symbiotic relationship that exists between the praise of the people and the proclamation of the prophet. We ought to all hunger for the Palm Sunday experience. Our text falls in the contextual framework of what scholars call the triumphal entry. Triumphant because Jesus was a winner even before he got to Jerusalem. Going through Jerusalem doesn't make you a winner. Having the courage to face it and the determination to go through it makes you a winner. A psycho analytical observation of the text makes one wonder what the mental framework and emotional stability of Jesus was as he marched towards the place he would die. Could it be that the frustrations, which evolved from the final destination on earth, caused him to leap off of the colt, run into the precincts of the temple and chase everyone out? Or perhaps it was a depression that arose from the depth of his heart and caused him to weep as he came closer to the gates of the city. With jealous preachers commenting that the whole world has gone after him, and the religious rank and file telling him to shut his disciples up, one wonders where he found the strength to deal with all of the dynamics of a shouting crowd amidst his inner turmoil.

Yet when exasperation mixes with expectation the end result is always exultation. How do you get your praise on in the sanctuary when you're coming from a spiritual insane asylum? How do you get your praise on at the annual conference when you don't know if your coming back to the appointment for another year?

How do you shout on the outside when you've been shot on the inside? It is due to the composite of exasperation mixed with expectation giving birth to exultation. Many Sundays I wished I had this crowd with me. Many days I wished I could go through the sermonic rolodex of time, and have them to do a workshop on how to have church. The question remains, *"What do I need to do in order to keep the consistent flow of the Palm Sunday experience in the service of worship*? How can 11:00 come alive? It's really in the text. First of all we discover that there must be a *distinct sound*. The text says they shouted. They shouted in the front of him, and they shouted in the back of him. The word shout conveys the idea that this was no silent and somber crowd. This was no liturgically confined group who was to bougie to make noise. This was no crowd that sat with their arms folded and legs crossed. They shouted!!!

The religious intelligentsia tried to tell Jesus to keep them quiet. Jesus didn't stop them from shouting. Jesus liked the noise that came from the crowd! Every Pastor ought to be warned. Don't be fooled by the pseudo practices of wanna be orthodox hypocrites. Don't allow anyone to throw water on the 12 alarm blazing fire of your passion. Don't allow the frozen chosen to lower the spiritual thermostat that warms your very soul. Don't get it twisted!! Jesus loves noise!!! I remember at one of my pastoral appointments, a woman came to me and suggested that the only reason why people shouted in church was because they were having personal problems. The impression that she was giving was that the shouting crowd was composed of those who were mentally psychotic and emotionally neurotic to the point that they had no other outlet save to act a bonnified fool in church.

Before I could really get angry with her, I had to think about what she said. While she said it from the wrong spirit, there was some truth to the matter. The Gospel of Luke said that the motley crowd was composed and comprised of people whom Jesus had both helped and healed. The crowd was comprised of people who Jesus cast devils from. One man in the crowd was raised from the dead. My dear confused member missed a pivotal point that is in the text. It wasn't because they where *delusional* that they shouted. It was because they were *delivered* that they shouted. Usually the ones who make the most noise in church are the ones that have been delivered from something.

The Lord loves noise. In heaven, the book of Revelation says, *"I heard what sounded like the voice of a great multitude, the roar of many waters and like the sound of mighty cracks of thunder, crying out, Hallelujah! For the Lord our God the Almighty reigns.*

Let us rejoice and exult and give him the glory for the marriage of the Lamb has come, and his Bride has made herself ready. It was granted her to clothe herself in fine linen, bright and pure for the fine linen is the righteous". The Lord loves noise! At his birth, the heavenly host made noise by singing *glory to God in the highest peace on earth and goodwill towards men.* The Lord loves noise!. He was born in noise...He died with noise... and in heaven is surrounded by noise! We discover that there is not only the need for a *district sound*, but there must be an understanding of *divine assignment.* What would our churches be like if they recognized that every time they showed up on Sunday morning they were on divine assignment. The text says they shouted blessed is he that comes in the name of the Lord. Every pastor ought to rhetorically ask the congregation, *"In who's name are you here today"*? The fact is that we wash up in the morning. We dress in our Sunday finest. However in who's name do we show up ? Other than HIS name, there are really two other names that you can show up in. An individual can show up in his or her own name. Many people show up at worship believing that they're doing God and the church a favor just for being there. As this person graces the cathedral with their presence, the trumpets ought to be blown, the spotlight ought to flash on them, and the audience ought to give them a standing ovation.

After all, they're on the deacon board. They're a trustee; they give a lot of money to the church. Their whole attitude is, *"They better recognize"*! They come in their own name. They have great singing voices. They are dynamic orators and sophisticated rhetoricians. They are great businessmen, or dynamic administrators. They come in their name. The other way is to come in the name of someone else. My dad went to this church. My mother started this church. My family was here before the pastor and they'll be here when the pastor is gone. The only problem is that my name, or my families name can't heal, deliver, and set free. The minuet that we step into the sanctuary we ought to understand that we are on assignment in the name of Jesus! I recall one year in school we were given an assignment.

We had to read a book and write a rather large paper on the book. Now I messed around and waited until the last minuet to do what I was supposed to do. I went out and played basketball. I went out to the movies. I went out on dates. One day before the paper was due, not having read hide nor hare of the book I said to my self, "*I need to get this book report done*". As I read the 150-page book, my eyes got extremely heavy. (My wife calls it the ole sleepy eye). I managed to flub my way through writing the report hoping to at least get a "c". The next week when I went to her office, my professor smiled at me and handed me my paper......with a big fat "F" on it!! I mentioned that because a whole lot of us are playing with this thing called worship. A whole lot of us are putting our clothes on, doing our hair, putting on perfume and cologne, only to come through the church doors to play church. We look suppressed when there's no one joining our church.

We get nervous when the financial resources dry up. We get sad when people leave the church, or when the pastor decides to leave. Its because we've wasted time in foolishness, and because of that we're getting bad grades in evangelism and out reach. However the minuet that our feet hit the sanctuary, we ought to remember that we are on assignment. Yes the preacher has the assignment of preaching. Yes the choir has the assignment of singing. But everyone has been given the assignment of praise. Our assignment is to throw those hands up to the glory of God. Our assignment is to triumphantly shout to the glory of his name! Our assignment is to thank him for keeping us one more day. The Palm Sunday experience is reflective of a community of believers who had a *distinct sound*. The Palm Sunday experience was reflective of those who realized that they were on *divine assignment*. Finally the Palm Sunday experience was reflective of those who *desired to be delivered*. The text says they shouted "***Hosanna,***" which means save or deliver now. The crowd was sociologically, historically and theologically astute enough to know that they needed to be delivered. Now in the context of this text, we discover that the cry for deliverance was sociological. Surrounded by the colonial oppression of the mighty Roman Empire the colonized cried out for salvation and deliverance. Palms were snatched from the trees to wave, and clothes were thrown on the ground because they thought that the dark child from Nazareth was going to be the conquering king to bring down the empires of men. Perhaps the empire was responsible for the dehumanization of colonized people of color by way of an overanxious pretoriate who killed first and asked questions later. Perhaps the unemployment rate was high among the colonized men of color forcing them to operate in the underground economy and employment. Perhaps the school system was inferior to other systems of education on the east side of Jerusalem. Perhaps the literacy level on the west side was low. Perhaps the drop out rates on the west side was high, and per haps no child left behind was a joke. Perhaps the infant mortality rate of the colonized was high, or perhaps the colonized had no health care. Perhaps the urban infrastructure was crumbling, perhaps Jobs were going overseas, or perhaps there were to many fake preachers who profiteered instead of prophesied. Perhaps there were Preachers who stood in the pulpit like the emperor who had on no pants... they cried out for deliverance! However the fact of the matter is that there is no outer deliverance, until there is inner deliverance. Herein is the heart of the problem at the 11:00 worship experience. Too many people sit in church not realizing that they need to be delivered. Some play the games of exclusivity ever harping on cliques and clubs in the household of faith. They need to be delivered. Too many get mad with the Preacher because he or she has backbone and refuses to be a pastoral flunky. When he/she refuses to be a pastoral flunky, they get mad and close up their pocketbook or wallet.

They need to be delivered. The quick condemnation and judgment of people that come to church and don't look smell or act like church ...a judgment that pushes them further and further away from the love of God. Church folk need to be delivered! Many worry about drive by bullets in the hood, what about the drive by tongues in the church? They need to be delivered! May I lean against that lamppost a little longer?

Surely you are aware that its not just unsaved people that need deliverance. Saved folk need deliverance. When you open your office door, put your briefcase down, sit at your desk in the front of a pink slip that boots you out of job, somebody ought to shout Hosanna!!

The young son that has been caught at the wrong place, at the wrong time, hanging out with the wrong crew gets thrown in jail ...somebody ought to shout Hosanna!! The parent who is left to take care of all of those children because their spouse didn't feel like staying at home.... somebody needs to shout Hosanna! I close with this. A young boy was feeling sick one palm Sunday and had to stay home from church. When his mom and his dad came home from church he noticed that they had a crisp palm in their hand. He asked, *"What is that in your hand"?* His dad explained, *"When Jesus showed up they laid down clothes and snatched palms off the tree to lay them before him".* The son said, *"awww shucks. The one Sunday I miss ...Jesus showed up".* If every Sunday is a Palm Sunday, then good church members don't want to miss a single Sunday. Why you ask? It's because when the crowd makes a distinct sound, when the crowd is on divine assignment, when the crowd desires deliverance, Then God shows up through the blessed Holy Ghost. When the Holy Ghost shows up, yokes are broken. When the Holy Ghost shows up, breakthroughs and breakouts happen. When the anointing shows up, preaching is made easy, singing is made sweet, as worship becomes fervent.

CHAPTER 10

Over The Wall or
Through The Door?

I am the door of the sheep, all that came before
me are thieves and robbers-John 10:7-8

What qualifies you to be a shepherd? Is it the process of ordination, which occurs at the annual conference? Is it the paper appointment that comes from the hand of the Episcopate? Is it the matriculation through institutions of higher learning? Is it because your daddy or your mommy was a preacher? What qualifies you as a pastor? Does it have to do with the fact that you were once a celebrity and now that qualifies you as a pastor? Does it have to do with the way you string your words together, or how you lace your theological assertions? What qualifies you to be a pastor? A dialogical event in the New Testament narrative sets the tone and the tenor of our text. The conversation piece evolves around the healing of a blind man. Jesus heals a blind man, and tells him to go and wash his eyes in the pool of Silom.

The healed brother goes, not realizing how much his healing is going to throw the religious status quo into an uproar. For In our text we discover that the Pharisees used their ecclesiastical authority to legitimize or delegitimized the healing ministry of Jesus the Christ. Nevertheless we soon discover that all of the rhetoric and oratorical probing, all of the practices of tradition, all of the philosophical and theological pontifications, are not enough to negate a blind man who can now see. The Pharisees forgot that theological dialogue must always be coupled by the practical proof in the pudding which is life transformation. The questions that the Pharisees asked were merely symptomatic of a deeper question...What qualifies and substantiates true and genuine leadership in ministry. In our text, the first set of Pharisaic questions represented a *stringent interrogation* of who did it. To the shock and chagrin of the Pharisees, it did not come from one who was a part of their religious clique. More precisely the question became, *"How did it happen without our hand"*. How could an unorthodox healing come from an unorthodox source? In my study of the New Testament narrative I am discovering that most of Jesus' ministry does not occur in the narrow confines of institutions of religious practice and profession. It was on the street that a woman was healed from an issue of blood. It was in Simons house that his mother was healed from a fever. It was in a funeral procession that a young man was brought back from the dead. It was on a boat that Peter was blessed with a massive catch of fish. Jesus' ministry went beyond the confines of institutional settings. At any rate the Pharisees moved from a stringent interrogation to a *negative declaration*...a negative declaration to say the least. Their conclusion was that whoever did this healing is a sinner.

He is not of God. He is an outsider or an interloper. In Short they said, *"Because he is not a part of us, because he doesn't practice or act like us, we choose not to accept this healing"*. They said this even though the healing was staring them straight in the face. Not much has changed in our time for there are many churches full of Pharisees that have rejected people that don't act like them and who are not caught up into church cliques. Many synagogues of Satan have run away preachers because the good Rev. choose not to be a puppy dog pastor, but a prophet that stands for truth no matter what it cost him or her. Yes, they moved from a stringent interrogation to a negative declaration. Yet from here the healed man gave a *powerful proclamation*. The healed man would dare to suggest that the nature of the healer determined the reality of what the healer could do. If he were not of God, he could do nothing. However because he was of God, he healed his blinded eyes. Needless to say, the stringent interrogation, the negative declaration, and the powerful proclamation caused an *unjustified excommunication*. The context says they threw the healed man out. They said, *"Who are you to argue with us? You're not a part of the interpreters of holy things. You're not educated. You're a sinner. You do wrong. You're not as sanctified as we are. You're not as churchy as we are"*.. And so in the context of our text the people are left confounded and confused around the question, "*What does qualified and effective leadership look like in the faith community*"? Does it have as Martin King put it; *high blood pressure when it comes to creeds but anemic when it comes to deeds*? Is it the one who has forgotten that in the words of Maugham *tradition is a guide but not a jailer*? Is it the one who doesn't understand that *exclusivity leads to extermination*? What does true leadership look like? In reality not only is it a question of true leadership, but also it is a question of what leadership method works in favor of the ones being led. How can you tell if one is a genuine leader of God in the household of faith? In 2016, the question hasn't gone anywhere. With all of the scandal surrounding church leaders and the way it has affected how we see ourselves and how others see us, the question yet looms, "*What does genuine and sincere church leadership look like*"? How can you tell a fake leader from a genuine leader? How can you tell the difference between one who was sent by God, or one who got in some other way. At the beginning of chapter ten Jesus clears up the confusion. In our text he says, "*I am the door of the sheep. All that came before me were thieves and robbers*. It is here that we note the two ways of getting to the sheep. One can either get to the sheep from over the wall, or one can get to the sheep through the door Wight in his book manners and customs of bible lands notes that thieves would sneak into the sheep fold by scurrying up and climbing over the wall. When they got into the fold they would cut the throat of the sheep and through the sheep over the wall. That is what Jesus is making reference to when he talks about gaining entrance to the flock some other way. The thief or the robber had only one objective. The objective was to use the sheep for their own selfish purpose. They really cared nothing about the sheep. They only wanted to use the sheep for what they could get out of the sheep. They were butchers for their own benefit. I must confess that as I read this passage, it disturbed me. It didn't disturb me because of the reality of its truth.

It disturbed me because over the years I always assumed that if an individual was in a pulpit they where there because God allowed them to be put there. I assumed that because it had a rather large following, and because it had notoriety it was because God wanted it to be that way. I had not discovered that there were two ways in which a man or a woman could become the pastor of a church. A person could climb over the wall. Leadership that is built upon the foundation of getting in another way(as opposed to the Jesus way) generally doesn't look out for the best interest of the pasture.

Every methodological approach and purpose only serves the interest of the rogue leader. Do understand that we are not just talking about pastoral leadership. This is also inclusive of lay leadership. The greatest challenge to pastoring is in administrating and organizing around officers who operate out of a sense of self-interest. The foundational interest is not to grow the church spiritually and numerically. The interest is not to support the vision of the God given visionary; the interest is not to be a living voice in a dying community, the interest centers around feeding the insatiable ego appetite of me, myself, and I. In dysfunctional churches this dynamic takes over during church meetings. The meeting looses its focus as the work of ministry becomes a stage or forum for the dysfunctional member, (or members) to act a fool. In the end, hours are wasted and no work is done. What pastor hasn't been there? At any rate we discover that there is good news in the text. Jesus says, *"I am the door"*. The door is symbolic of two realities. Primarily it is the symbol of acceptance. Acceptance means you are acceptable. One should always remember and never forget that there is a difference between our standards of acceptance and the Lords standard. There is a big difference between our understanding of whose leadership is accepted and the Lords qualifying process. Many books have been written in the area of practical theology about who or what the adequate qualifications of a good shepherd are. However the metaphorical and allegorical language of the text dares suggests to us that in the end the Lord determines who is legit. It is the Lord who qualifies or disqualifies. The chief shepherd gives access to the under shepherd because he or she has a genuine love for the Lords sheep. At the end of Johns Gospel we see Jesus looking into Peters eyes asking. *"Lovest thou me"*?. And then saying, *" feed my sheep"*. The foundation and chief qualification for having the door open is love for Gods sheep. At this level it doesn't matter whether it is a storefront, mid size or mega church. The fundamental criteria are not that you love the structure, not that you love the connection, not even the budget, but that you love the sheep. That is the inner password that allows you access into Gods most precious account; love for the sheep. Acceptable leadership must come through the door, and the door is Jesus Christ. There is something else in the text.

The door reflects the divine placement. When my dad was in the military, he was on orders to go over seas. He was on his way to Europe. However daddy didn't want to go overseas. He didn't want to move his family from Baltimore, and he didn't want to leave his Mother in York Pa. He decided to get out of the service and get another Job. The only problem was that this was not the will of God. Every Job he applied for didn't come through. When he tried to get a job in Kentucky it created a greater hardship on the family. With a college degree and a Masters of Divinity he ended up Pumping gas on Reisterstown road in Baltimore. He soon discovered that what God had done was shut the door on every opportunity save what God ultimately wanted him to do. God wanted him overseas. When he reapplied to get back in the service, the door flung wide open. In his own words he told me," *It was as though I never left*". He also shared with me that when God wants you in a specific place, he will shut all the doors around you, until you walk through **his** open door. The door is the symbol of divine placement and accepted leadership. When one goes through the door he or she is placed among the sheep. A door will not be opened to sheep that God does not want you to be among. Here is a lesson for the discouraged Baptist preacher who is upset because he didn't get the church that he did a candidacy for. For whatever reason God did not want you at that place and at that time. And so every pastor must ask themselves the question, *"has my leadership of this congregation passed through the door" Has the leadership model been divinely placed inside of me and is it acceptable to God*? Even after I accept the appointment, and observe the church, have I talked to God about the leadership approach and structure? Allow me to also suggest that most of my work in ministry has been in areas that I never really wanted to do ministry at. One church was on a dairy farm. Another was a church that was in turmoil. Another church threw me out.. Yet all through the journey I have been convinced and convicted that this is where the Lord needed me. The good news is that there is always one door that helps explain why God opened the other doors in your past. There is always one door that brings you the ah-ha moment. The door is reflective of divine acceptance, the door is reflective of divine placement and the door is reflective of divine preparation. Leadership must always be prepared through the door of Jesus Christ. The one thing that we will never get away from is the fact that no pastoring begins without adequate preparation. The idea here is that if you feel called to pastoral ministry, you have to go through the Jesus door. It is ideological that one goes through the training process of our mentor and elder brother in order to be effective in pastoral ministry and leadership. One goes through four years of college in order to be an expert in their given field of study. Every professional place of employment has on the job training in order to familiarize the new employee with the intricacies of the Job.

Every soldier must go through boot camp in order to be the best soldier they can be during the time of warfare. Pastoral ministry demands that the neophyte pastor go through the door called Christ. Many pastors will attest to the fact that pastoral ministry is not an easy Job. There will be times of wonderful acacceptance, but there will also be times of painful rejection. Going through the door called Jesus we have an adequate understanding of the rejection that he faced. Indeed he came among his own and his own received him not. However the "door" teaches us that if we remained focus we learn that while the world rejects us the one above the world accepts us. We learn that while there will be many who agree with us, there will be those who live and breath to make fools out of us. The bible teaches us that scribes and Pharisees followed him everywhere to set him up for failure. Yet the door teaches us that the door had an answer for every one of their accusations. We pastors are very much aware that in the church, many will be committed to the vision and mission of the church. On the other hand we discover that there will be some who betray you and turn on you. They will flip on you like ihop pancakes. However the door teaches us that we are to be committed to our purpose.

Many walked away from Jesus. Judas betrayed Jesus, Thomas doubted Jesus, and Peter denied Jesus. The amazing thing is that all of this transpired after Jesus spent time with them explaining the vision and the mission. Yet the door teaches us that sometimes you have to carry on with the vision and mission even though you may have to tote the way all by yourself. And so in developing our understanding of the Lord's ministry, we adequately prepare ourselves for life among the sheep. We are prepared to deal with those sleepless nights wondering if our world is turned upside down by the removal of an appointment. We are prepared to deal with standing before the congregation like Jesus stood before the crowd in the presence of Potions

Pilate. We are able to deal with the congregation who is refusing to pay the general claim in order to get rid of the pastor. We are able to deal with the insufficient salary, the long work hours, the treacherous travel, the weariness of the spirit and the pressure of family life all because the "door" has adequately prepared us. I close this sermon by suggesting that in verse 9 we have the aftermath and the blessing of the one, who is divinely accepted, divinely placed and divinely prepared. After the Lord reminds us that he is the door, he says that in him the sheep come in and go out. This means that the ones that are divinely accepted, the ones who are divinely placed and the ones who are divinely prepared are blessed to the point that the pasture or the pastorate has a sense of serene security. The phrase go in and come out is one that connotes a sense of safety, and if there is anything that the sheep of 2016 need is a safe pasture. We need pastorates safe enough to give God the praise, safe enough to grow closer and closer to Jesus, safe enough to find help when needed, and safe enough to grow young into the bosom of Abraham.

CHAPTER 11

The Good Shepherd

*"I am the good shepherd, the good shepherd
giveth his life for the sheep". John 10:11*

What kind of shepherd are you? What contextual framework do you use to define what a good shepherd is? It is a question that every serious preacher ought to ask him or herself. In the secret places of self reflection, in the quiet moments when you literally hold a mirror up to your soul, how do you answer the still small voice which raises up the self analytical inquiry...*what kind of shepherd are you?* The question evolves from and revolves around the context of our text. The sacred standard, and the example of excellence does tot come from seminary studies. The meaningful model does not come from the preaching polls of popular opinion. It is in John 10:11 that the chief shepherd gives us an understanding of what it means to be a good shepherd. You will notice that the goodness of the shepherd has nothing to do with the number of members.

Jesus didn't say that the good shepherd is the pastor of a mega church. You will notice that the goodness of the shepherd has nothing to do with the charisma of the pastor. Jesus did not say that the good shepherd has holy swagger. You will notice that the goodness of the shepherd has nothing to do with the financial wherewithal of the pastor. Jesus didn't say that the good shepherd is loaded. Jesus is very definitive in what constitutes a good shepherd. He is crystal clear, tenaciously transparent, and undeniably up front about what it means to be a good shepherd. In the wilderness of misunderstanding, in the desert of misinformation, and in the forest of theological chaos, the words of our Lord are definitive, direct, and descriptive regarding the elemental composite of what constitutes a good shepherd. Yet in our text we are rescued from ignorance by way of a Christological interpretation of a ecclesiastical function. With boldness in his tone, and authority in his voice he says, *"I am the good shepherd, the good shepherd gives his life for his sheep"*!

Its antecedent defines the preface of the conjunctional phrase. *I am the good shepherd; the good shepherd gives its life for the sheep.* Christological proclamation is broaden by theological reality. In a sense, Jesus says, *"Never mind me, It is the holy persona beyond this physiological frame that is referred to in the old covenant as "I am" that is the good shepherd.* I am! YAHWE is the good shepherd. God is the good shepherd. He shepherds the stars into the sacred places of a nocturnal night, and calls the sun to rise upon eastern horizons! God is the good shepherd! He calls the shoals of fish by name and leads them to their place of slumber. God is the good shepherd! He guides the lightning he pushes the wind, he moves the earth, all of nature are the sheep of his pasture...God is the good shepherd!! When one of his sheep goes into surgery the good shepherd is right there. When one of his sheep has to go to court, the good shepherd is there!

When one of his sheep gets evicted, because they couldn't come up with the rent...the good shepherd is there! Just when the sheep is ready to throw the towel in and give up, the good shepherd is there! God is the good shepherd! I dare say that there be some pastors who have forgotten that God is the good shepherd.

His pasture is the panoramic picture of your whole life. He is your shepherd Zion preacher. H is your shepherd Apostolic preacher. He is your shepherd Baptist preacher. When the frustrations of holding a God given vision that the congregation doesn't want to embrace, we resign not because God is our shepherd. When the building cost is high but the giving is low and slow, we faint not because God is our shepherd. When it gets lonely in the midnight hour, when no one is texting us, tweeting us or hitting us up on Facebook, we don't grow weary because God is our shepherd. Well the question is begged *what does a good shepherd do ?* Semantically reflecting upon the term shepherd, we are astute enough to know that the Latin translation of the word pastor is shepherd. What makes a good pastor? The revelation, which falls from the mouth of Jesus has found its way inscribed in our text. The good shepherd gives his life for the sheep. First of all we discover that a good pastor understands that his or her life is a gift given to God rather than a life that serves the self.

In Israel, the condition of the house was directly linked to shepherds who where more concerned about self than the community of faith. Isaiah talked about it *.His watchmen are blind: they are all ignorant, they are all dumb dogs, they cannot bark; sleeping, lying down, loving to slumber. Yea, they are greedy dogs, which can never have enough, and they are shepherds that cannot understand: they all look to their own way, every one for his gain, from his quarter.* Ezekiel talked about it. "*Thus saith the Lord GOD unto the shepherds; Woe be to the shepherds of Israel that do feed themselves! Should not the shepherds feed the flocks? Ye eat the fat, and ye clothe you with the wool, ye kill them that are fed: but ye feed not the flock. The diseased have ye not strengthened, neither have ye healed that which was sick, neither have ye bound up that which was broken, neither have ye brought again that which was driven away, neither have ye sought that which was lost; but with force and with cruelty have ye ruled them. And they were scattered, because there is no shepherd: and they became meat to all the beasts of the field, when they were scattered. My sheep wandered through all the mountains, and upon every high hill: yea, my flock was scattered upon all the face of the earth, and none did search or seek after them*" Jeremiah talked about it. *Woe be unto the pastors that destroy and scatter the sheep of my pasture saith the LORD. Therefore thus saith the*

LORD God of Israel against the pastors that feed my people; Ye have scattered my flock, and driven them away, and have not visited them: behold, I will visit upon you the evil of your doings, saith the LORD. The good shepherd isn't hung up on capitalistic interpretations of success. The good shepherd isn't caught up in the church joneses, where the emphasis is on who can build the biggest building. If they never put the good shepherds name in the paper, their ok with that. If they never get the opportunity to preach at the mega conference, their ok with that. If they don't travel in a multi million-dollar jet, or drive in a million dollar car, it doesn't matter.

They understand that their life is a sacrificial offering. They understand that their life is reflective of a willful and submissive vulnerability. They don't ask what can I get out of it, but they ask what can I put in it. It is a gift given to God rather than a life that serves the self. It is said that Cyrus, the founder of the Persian Empire, once had captured a prince and his family. When they came before him, the monarch asked the prisoner, "*What will you give me if I release you*"? "*The half of my wealth,*" was his reply. "*And if I release your children*"? "*Everything I possess.*" "*And if I release your wife?*" "*Your Majesty, I will give myself.*" Cyrus was so moved by his devotion that he freed them all.

As they returned home, the prince said to his wife, "Wasn't Cyrus a handsome man"! With a look of deep love for her husband, she said to him, "*I didn't notice. I could only keep my eyes on you, the one who was willing to give himself for me.*" The good shepherd understands that his or her life is a gift given to God rather than a life that serves the self. There is something else here. Good pastors not only discover that their life is a gift given to God rather than a life that serves the self.. They eventually learn that pastoring is a predetermined fate rather than the guarantee of acceptance. Mardquart discusses the irony of the passage. He notes that the pastures of Bethlehem herded sheep, which were to be used sacrificially for worship in the Jerusalem temple. Yet in this text the emphasis is not on the sacrifice of the sheep in worship. This emphasis is not about the sheep being sacrificed by the shepherd, it's about the shepherd being sacrificed for the sheep. In order to become a good shepherd the good shepherd must first become a lamb of God. When John saw Jesus coming to be baptized, he said," *Behold the lamb of God which taketh away the sins of the world".* He wasn't talking about an ordinary lamb. He had enough sense to understand the existential and preeminent purpose of Jesus. The universal pastorate of humanity would be given a shepherd who at the same time would become the sacrificial lamb, which would deliver dying sheep from the bony hand of death. His purpose was predetermined. His destiny was designated, and his path was preordained. It wasn't that everyone would love him It wasn't that every one would accept him. It wasn't that he would have no problems. His purpose was predestined. ***He was wounded for our transgressions, he was bruised for our iniquities: the chastisement of our peace was upon him; and with his stripes we are healed.*** It was predetermined. ***It was the LORD's will to crush him and cause him to suffer, and though the LORD makes his life an offering for sin, he will see his offspring and prolong his days, and the will of the***

LORD will prosper in his hand. It was predestined. ***The stone that the builders rejected became the chief cornerstone.*** It was predestined. Oh dear pastor, just because you received an appointment this year, that doesn't mean that you will rise on flowery beds of ease.

Just because you received a great appointment in the eyes of men, doesn't mean that the possibility of you being slaughtered in the pasture is gone. Its been predetermined that folks in the church will talk about you and call you everything but a child of God. However it's also predetermined that your resurrection is on the way. Paul helps us here by saying; *"I want to know Him, and the power of his resurrection and the fellowship of his suffering being made conformable unto his death"*! I want to be slaughtered so I can understand the power of getting back up again! And so we accept our predetermined fate. If God be for us, then who can be against us? We accept our predetermined fate. I will fear no man, for the Lord is my helper. I accept my predetermined fate, for the Lord is my shepherd and I shall not want. Ill accept my predetermined fate because yeah tho I walk through the valley and shadow of death I will fear no evil, thou art with me. Scroggie, in his commentary on the Psalms, tells the story of an atheist who wanted to persuade his young son with his philosophy of life, who much to his concern was getting interested in the Christian faith. The atheist father prepared this very attractive plaque and hung it on the wall where his son could see it everyday. This plaque said, "GOD IS NOWHERE." Misreading the plaque the young man said, *why that is exactly what we learned in Sunday school.*

DR. EDWARD B. SAXON

God- is- now- here"! I see something else here. A good shepherd not only understands their life is a gift given to God rather than a life that serves the self. They not only understand that pastoring is a predetermined fate rather than the guarantee of acceptance, They also understand that they operate out of a love that manifests itself in protection as oppose to a cowardice that manifest itself in self-preservation. Far be it from me to suggest that pastors shouldn't take care of themselves. Every pastor should have success as one reconstructs the understanding of what real pastoral success is according to Gods word. Necessity dictates this because there are some that are successful in salary and notoriety, but are horrible failures when it comes to pastoring people. All pastors should take care of themselves; as a fit pastor is fit to pastor. Far be it from me to suggest that pastors shouldn't care for themselves. However when the exclusive modis operand is self-preservation, pastoring becomes problematic. Good shepherds protect the sheep. In the acceding part of this verse the shepherd is juxtaposed and contrasted with the hireling. The difference between the two is in the response they have when the wolf shows up. The shepherd stays to fight, the hireling runs and hides. Zoological study helps us to understand the nature of what the shepherd fights against. Wolves usually travel in packs. When they hunt their very cooperative and unified with each other.

One of them puts the entire group of prey on the run. After this they look for the weakest prey and the hunt becomes focused on that particular one. When the weak one gets confused, and separates from the heard that's when they strike. The ironic

102

thing is that wolves always look for the bigger prey. And so if a shepherd got in the way of the hunt, they would devour the shepherd. Fra Joseph Horn helps us to imagine the nature of the shepherd wolf fight. He says, *"Imagine in your mind eye the following. In the background, a flock of sheep grazing in peace on rolling green hills, But in the foreground, we see a shepherd and a wolf grappling in bloody mortal combat. The wolf's jowls are dripping with blood as it ferociously lunges at the shepherd's throat. The shepherds' clothes are torn and bloody, as he is in obvious pain, but his face holds a mixture of anger and courageous determination. He is looking directly into the face of the wolf, and he reaches towards it ready to throw it to the ground. His hands are torn and bleeding and it is easy to see that the fight has been going on for a long time. But he is not giving up, and will not allow the wolf to get to the sheep".* As fierce as this descriptive depiction sounds, the battle becomes fierce when the wolf infiltrates the sheep. In a pastoral context, that is what pastor's deal with. It is not so much the ones that lurk around the out- side, it is the ones that have already made it in. It should be noted at this point, that contrary to connectional belief, its difficult to pastor a wolf *and* a sheep. I recall at one church, the wolves were on the hunt.

Spiritually I could see the drops of blood from innocent members dripping from their ravenous mouth. When we arrived at the meeting (which they established on their own) I looked for my under shepherds to sit with me, as I hoped together we would fight the wolves. At the beginning of the meeting all the under-shepherds left me to fight all by myself.

It was at that time that I realized the congregation had been corporately devoured. Immediately after that meeting I cleaned out my office and vowed never to return. It's difficult to pastor a wolf. The consensus is that if you love the wolf enough the wolf will magically transform his nature from a fierce carnivore to a meek sheep. It is true that transformation can happen. People do change. But wolves have to be fought while they are wolves; not only for the sake of the shepherd and the sheep but also for the life of the one that has the wolf spirit. Shepherds don't play tootsie with wolves. Wolves must be fought! This is not a matter of politicking and teaming up with the wolf to do ministry. When that happens the pastor forfeits his or her right to be called a shepherd. This is because of a love that manifests itself in getting bloody to protect the sheep! If the weapons of our warfare are not carnal but are mighty to the bringing down of strongholds, what's the sense of having the weapon if were not gong to use it. What's the sense of having a rod and a staff if we're not going to use it? It is no secret that many of our churches are in an uproar because we have aloud the wolves to sit up in church, and we have not brought the fight to the very ones who are turning the church upside down. Love will make you use your rod.

Love will make you protect the sheep from the outside in and from the inside out. It goes beyond mentioning that some pastorates will leave the pastor with scars. I am not referencing the pastor who doesn't care enough about the congregation to endure hurt. I am not referencing the pastor who spends so much time away from the flock that he has lost the necessary pathos of pastoring. I am talking to the pastor who is close enough to care. I am talking to the pastor who genuinely walks with the sheep. The one who is consistently involved in pastorate drama. I'm not talking to the one who Jesus refers to as the stranger who doesn't know the shepherd's voice. I'm talking to the one scarred. In Austria one of the most popular sport was fencing. With artistic poise the fencer would hold the sword up to his nose with the other hand behind his back. With the shout of "*on guard*," the clanging swords would meet. Eventually one of the combatants would receive what is commonly referred to as the mensur scars. The mensur scar was the badge of honor that you received from the fierce battle. You were somebody if you were scarred. I believe this is why doctors where stripes or bars on there graduation robe. You are recognized as being distinguished. Scars mean something. When Jesus was in the room with Thomas he showed him his scars. The scar from the wound identified him as Jesus. Scars mean something. Scars don't stop us, scars are the living proof of the love we have for Christ and his flock.

CHAPTER 12

Wait Before You Wag

And as they passed by reviled him,
wagging their head Mathew 27 :39

As the young Pastor stood in the pulpit to pray there was an eerie sense of sadness in the atmosphere. Everyone had known the debacle that had happened on the previous Sunday. Silently some said in their hearts, "*I'm just glad it aint me*", while others prayed "*God Keep him.*" Most had already known what the Episcopate was about to do; yet the Pastor lifting up the prayer didn't know what was happening. As he talked to many of his colleagues, there was a grim and woeful look upon their face that silently said, "*I know something you don't know*". The river of gossip flowed, the rumor mill levy broke, and heads began to wag. The scenario wasn't much different at Golgotha. To many, the ministry of the young preacher from Nazareth looked like a colossal failure. He disrupted the religious status quo of his day. He was not afraid to deal directly with his detractors. All of the members of his church left him. He was brought before the governor, and now he was hanging on a cross. As he hung on the cross, head waggers showed up. There is a connection between head waggers and cross hangers. It would seem that there is intellectual satisfaction and emotional stimulation when a head wagger perceives that someone else is worse off than them. Headwaggers are delusional in that they fail to realize misfortune can swoop up any of us, any time and at anyplace. Head waggers can never be revolutionary because they are confined to the context of the ordinary. Head waggers will always show up at the crucifixion, but will never show up at resurrection morning. They will always show up at Mars hill but never show up in the synagogue where Paul persuades the Jews and the Greeks. Head waggers always show up while your being dragged to Patmos prison rather than when you're teaching the little flock to love one another. Head waggers sit in your church on Sunday morning waiting to do the final rites over your ministry.....Ashes to ashes, dust to dust. However I have learned that head waggers ought to wait before they wag. They really ought to wait because the prospect of blessedness is through the process of pain. Malcolm Muggeridge would suggest that every thing he learned about life didn't come through happiness, but through the process of pain. One writer would suggest that there are no scars for happiness and we learn so little from peace. Head waggers could only see the nails impaled in his hands and feet. Head waggers could only see the bloody face. Head waggers could only see his convulsing body. However in all of that they were so limited in their perspective that they couldn't see God at work for a greater cause. Something good was going to come out of something bad. The story is told of a man and his daughter who went for a walk out in the woods. As they walked, they came upon an almost butterfly. It seems that the butterfly had one wing out, and was trying to get the other out. The man and his daughter looked on and the man tried to help the butterfly by loosening the cocoon. However when he did that the butterfly fell dead. The lesson he learned was that some people need the struggle of emergence to survive. Struggle does something for us. Pain is medicine for us. Head waggers could not see that God through Jesus Christ was reconciling the world back to himself. He was wounded for our transgressions. He was bruised for our iniquities. The chastisement of our sin was upon him. Isaiah 53:10 says, *"It pleased God to bruise him"*. Head waggers don't understand that something good is going to come from this bad! The Apostle Paul understood this. Look at what he writes in1 Corinthians 4:9-14 *For I think that God hath set forth us the apostles last, as it were appointed to death: for we are made a spectacle unto the world, and to angels, and to men. We are fools for Christ's sake, but ye are wise in Christ; we are weak, but ye are strong; ye are honorable, but we are despised. Even unto this present hour we both hunger, and thirst, and are naked, and are buffeted, and have no certain dwelling place; And labor, working with our own hands: being reviled, we bless; being persecuted, we suffer it:*

Being defamed, we entreat: we are made as the filth of the world, and are the off scourging of all things unto this day. I write not these things to shame you, but as my beloved".

There is purpose in our pain. No, head waggers don't understand that the prospect of blessedness comes through the process of pain. As I reflected on this text another thought came to mind. Head waggers don't understand that the place of resurrection is never the same place as crucifixion. We never rise up in the same place we go down at. This is one of the reasons why the angel of the Lord had to raise the very relevant question, "*Why look ye for the living among the dead*"? Head waggers have the tendency of looking for you on the places that they buried you in. What they don't seem to realize is that the preachers and pastors of Jesus Christ have resurrection power. They arise in different places that they went down at. The disciples that showed up in Galilee were there because they loved the Lord. They were happy because he was alive. Head waggers could have never shown up in Galilee because it would have shaken their expectation at its core. Only those who love you will be at your crucifixion and your resurrection. Only those that care about you will see you die and watch you come alive again.-And so, what do we say to the waggers? Tell them to wait! I was young but now I'm old and I've never seen the righteous forsaken nor his seed begging bread! Tell them to wait!! All things work together for good of those that love the Lord and are called according to his purpose! Tell them to wait!! They that wait on the Lord shall renew their strength, they shall mount up with wings of an eagle, they will run and not be weary, they will walk and not faint, Tell them to wait!! And so!!As the young Pastor stood in the pulpit to pray there was an eerie sense of sadness in the atmosphere. Everyone had known the debacle that had happened on the previous Sunday. Silently some said in their hearts, "*I'm just glad it aint me*", while others prayed "*God Keep him*". Most had already known what the Episcopate was about to do. Yet the Pastor lifting up the prayer didn't know what was happening. As he talked to many of his colleagues, there was a grim and woeful look upon their face that silently said, "*I know something you don't know*". The river of gossip flowed, the rumor mill levy broke, and heads began to wag. But what they didn't know was that God sent the preacher down to Georgia where he earned a Doctorate degree. He got a job working with at risk families. He and his wife bought a beautiful home. They put three of their sons through college. His wife became chair of her S.T.E.M department in middle school. What do you tell the head waggers? Tell them to wait!!

Printed in the United States
By Bookmasters